Editor
Walter Kelly, M.A.

Managing Editor
Ina Massler Levin, M.A.

Editor-in-Chief
Sharon Coan, M.S. Ed.

Cover Artist
Jessica Orlando

Art Coordinator
Denice Adorno

Imaging
Alfred Lau
James Edward Grace
Rosa C. See

Product Manager
Phil Garcia

Publisher
Mary D. Smith, M.S. Ed.

W9-CSY-608

Expository Writing

Grades 6–8

Written by

Michael H. Levin, M.A., N.B.C.T

Teacher Created Resources, Inc.
6421 Industry Way
Westminster, CA 92683
www.teachercreated.com
ISBN-1-57690-995-6
©2001 Teacher Created Resources, Inc.
Reprinted, 2005
Made in U.S.A.

Table of Contents

What Is Expository Writing?

❏ Expository writing is the most common type of writing that students will be doing in high school and college. It is essentially writing that explains or analyzes a topic. (The word *expository* is from the word *expose*, which means "to reveal.") Although explaining a topic can be done in a variety of ways, the most common method in expository writing is to use examples and specific details.

❏ Expository writing is meant to answer questions. What questions? The questions asked in the form of a thesis. If the thesis is "middle school is difficult since students are trying to learn at the same time they are becoming young adults," then the writer must answer why becoming a young adult is a difficult process, especially at the same time as getting a formal education. Expository writing must provide the facts.

❏ Expository writing has often been compared to a lawyer arguing a case. This is a valid comparison. A lawyer must state what he or she will prove. Then the lawyer must provide facts which state the reasons a jury should agree. A writer states his or her position in the form of a thesis statement in the first paragraph of an essay. Then the writer, like the lawyer, must provide proof in the form of examples and specific details to allow the reader to see that there is validity in the thesis.

❏ As students learn to write the expository essay, keep in mind that it takes many years of practice to do it easily. A lawyer spends years in school and then years on the job, perfecting the craft. We cannot expect skilled essay writing to happen overnight. The reason we practice in middle school is so we have a strong foundation to continue perfecting our writing in high school and then, perhaps, in college.

❏ This book contains many ideas and concepts about expository writing. The lessons are constructed to help make students better writers, to challenge students in a positive way, and to make the journey in writing an effective one.

Why Teach Expository Writing?

Assumptions:

1. Students will be writing mostly expository essays in high school.

2. Most English teachers will expect students entering high school to have background in the essay form.

3. Teachers of grades 6–8 are more interested in short but cohesive essays of 250–300 words that demonstrate a competence with the form, rather than longer papers of over 400 words which are less tightly formed.

4. Teachers of grades 6–8 feel that constant practice of the expository form will yield better results than writing only a few essays.

5. Teachers of grades 6–8 are teaching the writing process.

6. Teachers of grades 6–8 constantly model what they expect the students to do.

7. Teachers of grades 6–8 expect to start teaching expository writing by having students write cohesive paragraphs.

8. Teachers will want to teach different forms of expository writing, including illustration and example, comparison and contrast, cause and effect, argumentative, and personal.

9. Teachers want to teach recursively, with each form echoed in succeeding exercises.

10. Teachers want students to feel comfortable with their ability to try all exercises.

11. Teachers of grades 6–8 feel that grammatical accuracy is but one important component of fluency in the expository form.

12. Teachers of grades 6–8 with access to computers expect their students to be able to word process their expository writing.

13. Teachers feel that by the time students leave eighth grade they should be able to write a multi-paragraph research paper of three or four pages.

14. Teachers know that writing fluency comes with continual practice in a setting where students' confidence can grow.

4

Classroom Atmosphere

"I hear and I forget. I see and I remember. I do and I understand."

—Confucius

❏ A teacher needs to make the classroom conducive for students to have an opportunity to understand. Look around the room. Consider the atmosphere for the maturity of your students and their ages. Is there stimulation? We want them to think, but too often we ask them to do so without providing the climate that encourages thinking. When students walk into your room, do they feel the surroundings are special? Can they see that you expect them to do great work, not only by what you say but also by the environment you have created?

❏ Some students who only want to *hear* will not expect to create. They will only listen halfheartedly to directions and then forget what they are expected to do. Make creativity a watchword in your classroom by providing students with a place where they want to write.

❏ Other students will *see* what you are trying to do and will perhaps remember something of your ideas. They will look but not make the transition to creation. Model what you want them to do. This book is filled with paragraphs and essays which will help your students to remember what they need to do.

❏ Make your students *do*. How is this done? One way is to show enthusiasm for your subject. Another is to join in on the assignments. Show them that writing is for everybody. Do for them, and they will do for you. They surely will understand what you want them to know.

❏ And lastly, remember that it takes many practice assignments to make a lesson one's own. Can you juggle? Yes, you can if you learn this skill by hours of practice. There will be many dropped balls and much frustration. However, if you stick with it, you can learn. Although it's hard to remember a time when you couldn't write, there was such a time. Rummage through your early writing and share it with the class. They will appreciate seeing how far you have come. And it will remind you that writing, like juggling, doesn't happen in a day.

Success will take many hours of doing, but like anything worthwhile the rewards are sweet when finally achieved.

"We are what we repeatedly do. Excellence, then, is not an act, but a habit."

—Aristotle

The Writing Journal

Students need to write every day. One way to get them going is to provide a journal topic to write about during the first five minutes of the period. While you take roll and do other necessary preliminary chores, the students can be productively writing.

Teachers often have trouble thinking of journal topics. Don't try so hard. Here are some ideas you can use each week. Stick with this, and soon the students will know what day of the week it is by the kind of inspiration they are given. Make sure your overhead projector is in working condition and . . .

❏ **Monday**—Show students a cartoon from the newspaper. After they have read it, have them comment on the ideas presented. What is the cartoonist trying to say? What was he thinking when he drew this? What does it make you consider in your life? (It's great to start the week off with a laugh. Your students will start asking for their "Monday morning joke." It will make you feel better about Monday morning, too!)

❏ **Tuesday**—Show students a transparency of a painting or sculpture. Many of these can be found in the teacher materials that come with textbooks. Tell them not to write anything for two minutes—just study the art. Then they can consider these things: What is happening in the painting? What was the artist thinking about when creating the piece? What does it make you consider in your life?

❏ **Wednesday**—Put up a quotation or proverb. There are hundreds of pithy ones. You could probably start today and not repeat one until the day you retire. You don't need to explain it. Perhaps a well-phrased question under it will get them going.

"Nothing great was ever achieved without enthusiasm."

—Emerson

Why does a person do better when he or she enjoys what is being done? What are you enthusiastic about?

The Writing Journal *(cont.)*

❑ **Thursday**—Display photographs of natural scenes. It is expensive to make transparencies of photographs, so you may want to start collecting calendars. Try looking around January 15th when the bookstores are practically giving them away. The day-to-day types have smaller pictures. Paste them on separate pieces of construction paper and pass them around. The one each student gets is the one he or she must connect to and write about.

Why would you like to visit this place or why not? What thoughts come to you as you study this photograph? Where do you think the photographer was when he took this? Describe the subject, using as many sensory words as you can in two minutes.

❑ **Friday**—It's Friday. Hooray! Time for something different!

Play a piece of music. Show a TV commercial. Share a family slide. Have students bring in a photograph or other "stimulator."

Give your students the opportunity to let their minds wander. Tell them that inspiration is just that. It is supposed to inspire them to write whatever they think about. There is no right response—except a "write" one!

Now how can a teacher read all of the journals? There is no need to. When you are ready to collect them, have each student choose two or three for you to read. Have the students put a star next to those and read only those. If you want to read one at random, tell them you will do this. Finally, if there are any they do not want you to read, have them put an "X" in the margin and, of course, respect their wishes. Make a comment about each one you read. They will appreciate reading these responses. Make the kinds of comments you would want them to make on your writing. Journals should be the one time you write only positive comments. Enjoy that opportunity.

Expository Writing Thought Questions

Answer the following questions, place them in your journal, and share responses with your classmates.

1. What has happened in the last week that has . . .
   - made you smile? _____
   _____
   - made you get angry? _____
   _____
   - kept you awake at night?_____
   _____
   - stayed on your mind?_____
   _____
   - made you daydream?_____
   _____

2. What is happening in the world that interests you? _____
   _____

3. What are some of the questions that your community faces?_____
   _____

4. What causes people you know to . . .
   - enjoy life? _____
   - seek the truth? _____
   - want to change? _____
   - make new friends?_____

5. Where is your favorite place to vacation? (*Expand with three reasons.*) _____
   _____

6. Why do you like (or dislike) the place you live? (*Give three reasons.*) _____
   _____

7. Write down your thoughts about the following:
   - pets_____
   _____
   - movies _____
   _____
   - TV shows_____
   _____
   - cars_____
   _____

Journal Cover

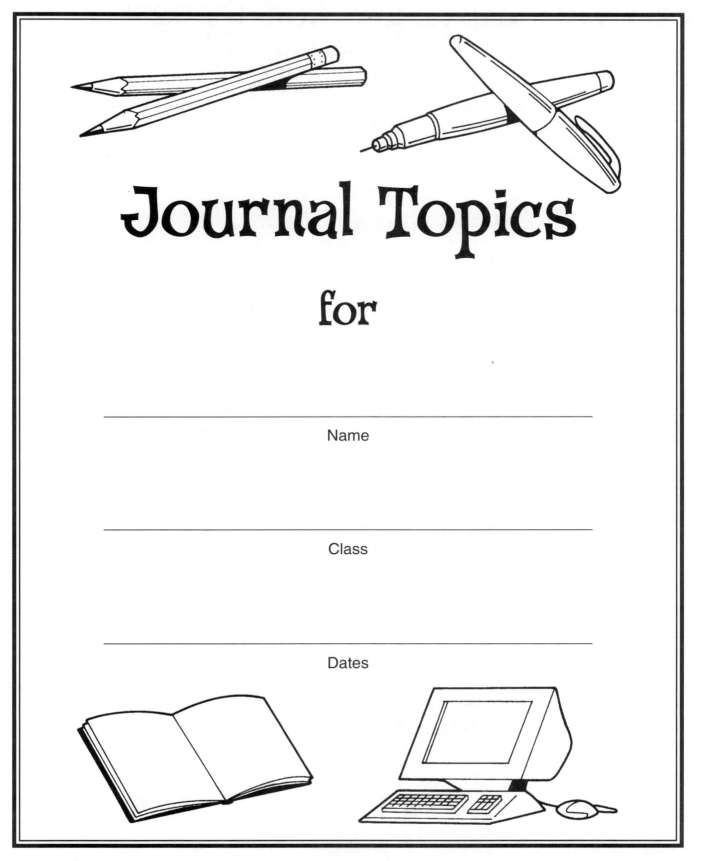

Journal Topics

for

_____

Name

_____

Class

_____

Dates

The Writing Portfolio

If at all possible, keep a portfolio for each student in the room. It need only be manila folders stored in a crate if you are short on space. The students will feel a sense of accomplishment as they watch their portfolios get thicker as the year progresses. By spring they will laugh with delight as they compare their early efforts with the "mature" writing they are doing now.

Make sure that students date their entries. They should keep the various stages of the writing process for a particular piece together. They can write a reflective essay about their favorite piece.

With computers becoming more prevalent in student homes and the classroom, it is becoming easier to send home copies of the work and also have ones for the portfolio. As students come in with computer skills, they may wish to use the computer to word process their work. Have them save separate drafts of each piece they do. All they need to do is title each draft the same but with numbers or letters added to show the progression (for example, *Trial Essay 1A*, *Trial Essay 1B*, etc.). If students are sophisticated enough, they may also want to use graphic organizers that they create and have filled in before beginning to write.

You can opt to send home a disk or have students print out copies of the materials that are part of their portfolios. Since most professional writers are using computers, it is a great opportunity to develop your students' keyboarding and general computer skills.

Writing Portfolio

The Writing Process

Prewriting

Much of the work in the writing process is done in the prewriting stage. The first step is thinking: an assignment is given or expository topics are brainstormed, and before the pencil meets the paper, ideas, thoughts, words, and memories flow through the mind. Chances are that one idea will escape and end up somewhere near the writer's heart; it is this idea that lingers. Later, passing between classes, during lunch, or walking home from school, the student finds this idea growing and taking shape in the mind. That is the one that will find its way to paper in a fully expressed essay.

Before writing, students should make personal connections to the topic. By reflecting on memories and events and recalling them as if they happened yesterday, the student will find the topic awakens. Since the topic is to be nonfiction, students should list what they know and what they do not know. Check the basic information and find the topic's worth. Bring it to life for others. If the idea is based on reading, students need to put themselves into the situation to empathize with others facing similar circumstances and events.

Ideas for prewriting include brainstorming; free-writing; listing who, what, when, where, why, and how; questioning; creating a bubble graph or outlining; asking and answering questions; listing the parts of the proposed essay—beginning, middle, end; and identifying thesis statements, controlling ideas, and supporting statements. All this amounts to a big task, of course, but remember that the more effort put into prewriting tasks, the easier the expository essay writing will be.

Compare the prewriting stage to preparing a garden. One cannot merely throw down seeds or buy established plants, put them in the ground, and then expect the results to look like the illustrations in gardening catalogs. First, a plan is needed. The type of garden, garden location, quality of soil, germination time, water and sunlight—these elements all affect the quality of the garden. Planning a garden is challenging. If the right plants or locations are not chosen, the plants will not achieve optimum growth. On the other hand, planning a garden is fun, and the rewards can be great.

Writing

Seeds and flowers are planted according to a plan. Nature cannot be expected to do the rest. Although the plants may be thriving in their new home, over-watering, lack of fertilizer, or under-watering can affect the plants' health and survival. This parallels the second stage of the writing process—in this case, the actual writing of an expository essay.

Up to this point, students have brainstormed; jotted down ideas; and created thesis statements, controlling ideas, and support examples. Information has been gathered and outlined sequentially.

It is now time to write! Let the words flow, creating a beginning, middle, and end. Now the essay has been completed.

If the completed writing does not seem to have any direction, the thesis statement is not clear, or the support is not strong, then perhaps the essay needs attention. The writer needs to stop and think. Does he or she care about the writing? Does it seem worth doing? If the answer is "Yes," then there is need to take a break and look at the essay with fresh eyes.

The Writing Process *(cont.)*

Revising

A garden grows, just as an essay develops and emerges. Is the process over? No. A garden will flourish, but some flowers will need to be thinned, and some areas will be sparsely filled. The next step is to grab a trowel and dig. Rearrange here and there, check for bugs, cut out spent flowers, and put mulch down to prevent weeds.

At the revision stage with an essay, the job is to add, omit, read, reread, and share with friends, classmates, teachers, and family to elicit comments and suggestions. The more feedback, the better— but remember that it is impossible to make everyone happy. So remember who the writing is for (that is, the intended audience) and take advice, but consider the source.

Editing

Editing is the next stage of the writing process, and it is similar to weeding. The essay has been revised, and now is the time to proofread it for errors, the weeds that may weaken the work. Misspelled words, sloppy punctuation errors, and overall laziness can make a good essay bad. It is good to take pride in the hard work and effort put into expository writing.

As for the garden, it is now maintenance time! Weed, water, and fertilize to keep it in top-notch form. A great deal of time and effort has been invested, and the support of a careful gardener is needed.

Publishing

Now is the time to display the expository writing! Be proud, smile, and share the essay that has involved so much energy, patience, and dedication. Essays can be presented to the class, e-mailed to friends and family, illustrated, word-processed, displayed on a bulletin board, or stuck on the refrigerator. Publishing is the stage of the writing process that allows the author to earn the reputation he or she deserves.

As for the garden—congratulations! The work has been entered in the garden show, and the green-thumb statue is on the family bookshelf. Flowers, vegetables, and herbs provide beauty, food, and a haven for butterflies, ladybugs, and bees. Admire the garden that took so much time and planning. Everyone else will too.

Gardening and expository writing are similar enterprises. Hard work reaps great rewards!

Standards for Writing
Grades 6–8

Accompanying the major activities of this book will be references to the basic standards and benchmarks for writing that will be met by successful performance of the activities. Each specific standard and benchmark will be referred to by the appropriate letter and number from the following collection. For example, a basic standard and benchmark identified as **1A** would be as follows:

> **Standard 1: Demonstrates competence in the general skills and strategies of the writing process**
> **Benchmark A: Prewriting:** Uses a variety of prewriting strategies (e.g., makes outlines, uses published pieces as writing models, constructs critical standards, brainstorms, builds background knowledge)

A basic standard and benchmark identified as **4B** would be as follows:

> **Standard 4: Gathers and uses information for research purposes**
> **Benchmark B:** Uses the card catalog to locate books for research topics

Clearly, some activities will address more than one standard. Moreover, since there is a rich supply of activities included in this book, some will overlap in the skills they address, and some, of course, will not address every single benchmark within a given standard. Therefore, when you see these standards referenced in the activities, refer to this section for complete descriptions.

Although virtually every state has published its own standards and every subject area maintains its own lists, there is surprising commonality among these various sources. For the purposes of this book, we have elected to use the collection of standards synthesized by John S. Kendall and Robert J. Marzano in their book *Content Knowledge: A Compendium of Standards and Benchmarks for K–12 Education* (Second Edition, 1997) as illustrative of what students at various grade levels should know and be able to do. The book is published jointly by McRel (Mid-continent Regional Educational Laboratory, Inc.) and ASCD (Association for Supervision and Curriculum Development). (Used by permission of McRel.)

Language Arts Standards

1. Demonstrates competence in the general skills and strategies of the writing process
2. Demonstrates competence in the stylistic and rhetorical aspects of writing
3. Uses grammatical and mechanical conventions in written compositions
4. Gathers and uses information for research purposes

Standards for Writing
Grades 6–8 *(cont.)*

Level III

1. Demonstrates competence in the general skills and strategies of the writing process

   A. Prewriting: Uses a variety of prewriting strategies (e.g., makes outlines, uses published pieces as writing models, constructs critical standards, brainstorms, builds background knowledge)

   B. Drafting and Revising: Uses a variety of strategies to draft and revise written work (e.g., analyzes and clarifies meaning, makes structural and syntactical changes, uses an organizational scheme, uses sensory words and figurative language, rethinks and rewrites for different audiences and purposes, checks for a consistent point of view and for transitions between paragraphs, uses direct feedback to review compositions)

   C. Editing and Publishing: Uses a variety of strategies to edit and publish written work (e.g., eliminates slang; edits for grammar, punctuation, capitalization, and spelling at a developmentally appropriate level; proofreads using reference materials, word processor, and other resources; edits for clarity, word choice, and language usage; uses a word processor to publish written work)

   D. Evaluates own and others' writing (e.g., applies criteria generated by self and others, uses self-assessment to set and achieve goals as a writer, participates in peer response groups)

   E. Uses style and structure appropriate for specific audiences (e.g., public, private) and purposes (e.g., to entertain, to influence, to inform)

   F. Writes expository compositions (e.g., presents information that reflects knowledge about the topic of the report, organizes and presents information in a logical manner)

   G. Writes narrative accounts (e.g., engages the reader by establishing a context and otherwise developing reader interest; establishes a situation, plot, persona, point of view, setting, and conflict; creates an organizational structure that balances and unifies all narrative aspects of the story; uses sensory details and concrete language to develop plot and character; excludes extraneous details and inconsistencies; develops complex characters; uses a range of strategies such as dialogue, tension or suspense, naming, and specific narrative action such as movement, gestures, and expressions)

   H. Writes compositions about autobiographical incidents (e.g., explores the significance and personal importance of the incident, uses details to provide a context for the incident, reveals personal attitude towards the incident, presents details in a logical manner)

   I. Writes biographical sketches (e.g., illustrates the subject's character using narrative and descriptive strategies such as relevant dialogue, specific action, physical description, background description, and comparison or contrast to other people; reveals the significance of the subject to the writer; presents details in a logical manner)

   J. Writes persuasive compositions (e.g., engages the reader by establishing a context, creating a persona, and otherwise developing reader interest; develops a controlling idea that conveys a judgment; creates and organizes a structure appropriate to the needs and interests of a specific audience; arranges details, reasons, examples, and/or anecdotes persuasively; excludes information and arguments that are irrelevant; anticipates and addresses reader concerns and counter-arguments; supports arguments with details and evidence, citing sources of appropriate information)

Standards for Writing
Grades 6–8 *(cont.)*

K. Writes compositions that speculate on problems/solutions (e.g., identifies and defines a problem in a way appropriate to the intended audience, describes at least one solution, presents logical and well-supported reasons)

L. Writes in response to literature (e.g., anticipates and answers a reader's questions, responds to significant issues in a log or journal, answers discussion questions, writes a summary of a book, describes an initial impression of a text, connects knowledge from a text with personal knowledge)

M. Writes business letters and letters of request and response (e.g., uses business letter format; states purpose of the letter; relates opinions, problems, requests, or compliments; uses precise vocabulary)

2. Demonstrates competence in the stylistic and rhetorical aspects of writing

A. Uses descriptive language that clarifies and enhances ideas (e.g., establishes tone and mood, uses figurative language)

B. Uses paragraph form in writing (e.g., arranges sentences in sequential order, uses supporting and follow-up sentences)

C. Uses a variety of sentence structures to express expanded ideas

D. Uses some explicit transitional devices

3. Uses grammatical and mechanical conventions in written compositions

A. Uses simple and compound sentences in written compositions

B. Uses pronouns in written compositions (e.g., relative, demonstrative, personal, [i.e., possessive, subject, object])

C. Uses nouns in written compositions (e.g., forms possessive of nouns, forms irregular plural nouns)

D. Uses verbs in written compositions (e.g., uses linking and auxiliary verbs, verb phrases, and correct forms of regular and irregular verbs)

E. Uses adjectives in written compositions (e.g., pronominal, positive, comparative, superlative)

F. Uses adverbs in written compositions (e.g., chooses between forms of adjectives and adverbs)

G. Uses prepositions and coordinating conjunctions in written compositions (e.g., uses prepositional phrases, combines and embeds ideas using conjunctions)

H. Uses interjections in written compositions

I. Uses conventions of spelling in written compositions (e.g., spells high-frequency, commonly misspelled words from appropriate grade-level list; uses a dictionary and other resources to spell words, uses common prefixes and suffixes as aids to spelling; applies rules for irregular structural changes)

J. Uses conventions of capitalization in written compositions (e.g., titles: books, stories, poems, magazines, newspapers, songs, works of art; proper nouns: team names, companies, schools and institutions, departments of government, religions, school subjects; proper adjectives: nationalities, brand names of products)

Standards for Writing
Grades 6–8 *(cont.)*

K. Uses conventions of punctuation in written compositions (e.g., uses exclamation marks after exclamatory sentences and interjections; uses decimal points in decimals, dollars and cents; uses commas with nouns of address and after mild interjections; uses quotation marks with poems, songs, and chapters; uses colons in business letter salutations; uses hyphens to divide words between syllables at the end of a line)

L. Uses standard format in written compositions (e.g., includes footnotes; uses italics for titles of books, magazines, plays, movies)

---

4. Gathers and uses information for research purposes

A. Gathers data for research topics from interviews (e.g., prepares and asks relevant questions, makes notes of responses, compiles responses)

B. Uses the card catalog to locate books for research topics

C. Uses the *Reader's Guide to Periodical Literature* and other indexes to gather information for research topics

D. Uses a computer catalog to gather information for research topics

E. Uses a variety of sources to gather information for research topics (e.g., magazines, newspapers, dictionaries, schedules, journals, directories, globes, atlases, almanacs)

F. Determines the appropriateness of an information source for a research topic

G. Organizes information and ideas from multiple sources in systematic ways (e.g., time lines, outlines, notes, graphic representations)

H. Writes research papers (e.g., separates information into major components based on a set of criteria, examines critical relationships between and among elements of a research topic, integrates a variety of information into a whole)

Creating Your Own Rubric

How Do I Begin?

First of all, it is important to know that your prompt or task and your rubric are part of the same package. Secondly, it is vital to realize that this is an interactive procedure—you will write, try out, and revise your prompt/rubric package until it tells you what you really want to know. Using standards-based activities like those in this book is a big help, but getting rubrics exactly right the first time is usually a result of experience.

Write the Rubric First

It is probably easiest to write the rubric first. A three-point rubric is the easiest, and you can begin at any point. The three-point rubric parts parallel one another and reflect different levels of the same skills. The "High Pass" contains all of the features of the "Pass," either in identical form or at a more advanced variation. "Needs Revision" considers parallel features, but they may be expressed as negatives.

Decide what you will be assessing in your rubric. Once you have decided what to include in your rubric, all criteria must appear in some form in all of the points.

Write the Prompt

Your prompt should be written to elicit a response that will allow assessment of the points in your rubric. If your "High Pass" requires the students to write more than one complete sentence, you should not instruct them to write "a sentence." This seems really obvious, but sometimes you will not catch this kind of thing until you are reading a batch of papers. If you suddenly realize that you are not getting any "High Pass" papers, you may want to look back at the wording of your prompt.

Revise, Revise, Revise

There are many results that might require you to revise your rubric and/or prompt. Look for some of these:

1. No high papers
   —Did I require something I have not taught?
   —Did I require something in the rubric that was not on the prompt?

2. All high papers
   —Did I want this result? (Is it possible for everyone to do really well?)

3. No passing papers
   —Were the directions wrong or easy to misinterpret?
   —Was the format different from our usual assignments?

4. Results inconsistent with the way I see my class
   —Do I need to look at the prompt/rubric package?
   —Do I need to take another look at the class?

Rubrics Are Power

Feeling comfortable with rubric writing gives you a powerful position in the assessment process. You will nearly always be able to justify your results and demonstrate how you obtained them.

Creating Your Own Rubric *(cont.)*

Use this blank form to create your own scoring rubric for a writing sample.

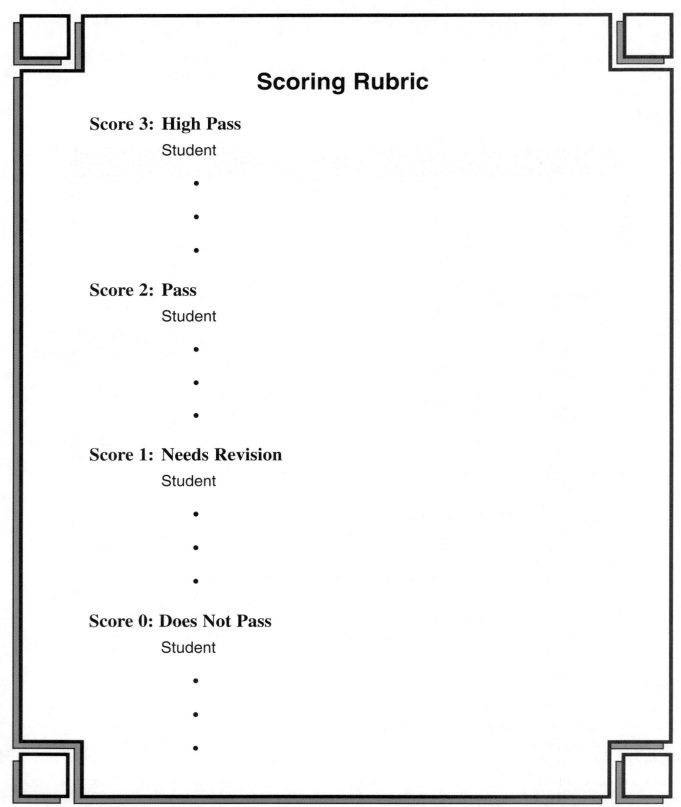

Scoring Rubric

Score 3: High Pass
Student

-
-
-

Score 2: Pass
Student

-
-
-

Score 1: Needs Revision
Student

-
-
-

Score 0: Does Not Pass
Student

-
-
-

Editing and Proofreading Marks

Editing Marks

Editing is the last stage before rewriting a paper for publication. Careful attention is paid here to removing grammatical and spelling errors. Universal editing marks are valuable because the same mark in an English classroom in Maine means the same thing in Wisconsin, Texas, and Alaska. Of course, you may develop your own marks or styles for personal revisions. In peer revisions, however, it is important to use universal marks. Use the chart below as your guide to these universal editing and proofreading marks.

Editor's Mark	Meaning	Example
ℓ	Delete	It was was very tiny.
≡	Capitalize	the boy ran quickly.
/	Use lowercase	Many Athletes ran in the marathon.
∧	Insert a word	I want an ice cream sundae.
RO	Run-on sentence	Who's there What do you want?
frag.	Sentence fragment	Although the peddler's cart. frag.
SP	Spelling error	Monkies swung in the trees.
∽	Reverse letters or words	Five books on were the shlef.
⊙	Add a period	Children played all day⊙
∧	Add a comma	I like apples peaches, and pears.
∨	Add an apostrophe	John's puppy is cute.
⌄⌄ ⌄⌄	Add quotation marks	Help! cried.
¶	Begin a new paragraph	"Hello," said Carla. "Hi," Beth replied.
#	Make a space	I love Frenchfries.
⌣	Close the space	He lives in the country side.
stet	Do not delete (Let it stand.)	The beautiful swan flew away.

Revising

Ultimately, you are the boss of your writing. However, letting parents, teachers, friends, and classmates read your essay will offer insights that perhaps you cannot see. Sometimes you know an essay in your own head and can picture the ideas, but maybe the essay doesn't paint a clear picture for readers. Giving others the opportunity to review your writing will enable you to discover whether others understood and enjoyed it.

Standards and Benchmarks: 1A, 1B, 1F

Introduction to Expository Paragraphs

- What is a paragraph? You could say a paragraph is a group of sentences. When handwritten, the first word of each paragraph is indented. When word processed, block style is generally used.

- Is there anything else you can add about this group of sentences? You could ask how they are related? How should a paragraph begin or end?

- What makes a good paragraph? Does it have to do with how many sentences are in it? If so, how many sentences are necessary, or how many are best?

These are some of the questions you should be able to answer in order to write good paragraphs.

You may have learned that a paragraph is defined as a group of sentences that develop one main idea. The one main idea is called a topic. This topic is what the paragraph is about. Read the following paragraph about an amusement park.

> Some amusement park rides, like rollercoasters, can be frightening experiences. Looking at a rollercoaster from the ground can make you think it is fun. However, once you are up in the air, your feelings can change. The coaster goes higher than you thought. The cars bump and swerve around so you feel as if you are about to fall out. Going to an amusement park is enjoyable, but it might be scary, too.

A paragraph usually begins with a topic sentence. In the paragraph above, the topic sentence is this:

> *Some amusement park rides, like rollercoasters, can be frightening experiences.*

This topic sentence can be divided into two elements. Besides having a topic, it also has an idea or attitude about the topic. This idea or attitude is called a *controlling idea* or the main point.

- **The topic**—amusement park rides

- **The controlling idea**—frightening experience

A paragraph that develops this topic sentence must explain why some amusement park rides are frightening. The clear development of the controlling idea is what makes an expository paragraph a good one.

- Expository writing explains or analyzes a topic.

- The word *expository* comes from the term *expose* which means "to reveal."

Standards and Benchmarks: 1A, 1B, 1F

Introduction to Expository Paragraphs *(cont.)*

Exposing a topic can be accomplished in many ways, but in expository writing it is usually done by supplying specific details and examples. In the amusement-park-ride paragraph, the writer explains why a ride might be frightening by supplying specific details about a rollercoaster. This is not the only way to reveal the controlling idea of frightening. The writer could have chosen to discuss another type of ride, such as one that uses a parachute to drop one from an extremely high point. That, of course, would have required different specific details or examples to expose the controlling idea and make the meaning clear to the reader.

In the space below on this page, see if you can use the same topic and controlling idea in a paragraph of your own about a different kind of amusement park ride. Remember to use specific details.

_____

_____

_____

_____

_____

_____

_____

_____

_____

_____

_____

_____

Introduction to Expository Paragraphs *(cont.)*

There can be many other ways to develop a paragraph about amusement park rides. Look at this example of a different topic sentence.

One of the best things about amusement parks is that everyone is in a happy mood.

Look to see if it has a topic and controlling idea.

- **The topic** is . . . *"best things about amusement parks."*
- **The controlling idea** is . . . *"everyone is in a happy mood."*

Without a controlling idea the topic sentence would have no main idea or attitude. Without a clearly stated topic, on the other hand, the main idea might seem unconnected or vague. If the writer, for example, had written "There is one best thing about amusement parks," the reader might still be uncertain (*what* is the best thing?) about what this paragraph was attempting to prove. The writer, too, might be uncertain about how to continue.

Now that we have a well-stated expository topic sentence, the controlling idea must be proved. Let's brainstorm some examples which show that people of all ages are in a happy mood at an amusement park.

1. Children are running around grinning and screaming with joy.
2. Teenagers are racing and laughing on the way to their favorite thrill ride.
3. Parents are acting like little kids, eating cotton candy and corn dogs.
4. Grandparents look at their grandchildren with approving smiles.
5. Even the ticket attendants seem to be smiling and pleasant.
6. The performers in costumes all act happy-go-lucky, without a care in the world.

Would these ideas support the controlling idea? Why?

_____

_____

_____

_____

_____

On the next page, write a paragraph using this topic sentence:

One of the best things about amusement parks is that everyone is in a happy mood.

You can use some or all or the supporting ideas listed on the page above. Make sure that all of your sentences are complete.

Standards and Benchmarks: 1A, 1D, 1F, 2B, 3A

Introduction to Expository Paragraphs *(cont.)*

Topic: Amusement Parks

Topic Sentence: *One of the best things about amusement parks is that everyone is in a happy mood.*

How did you do? Check to see whether each of your supporting sentences answers or supports the controlling idea.

How did you end the paragraph? Was there a sentence that summed up what came before? This is called a *conclusion*. When we write a paragraph, the conclusion comes in the last sentence. When we write an essay of four to six paragraphs, the conclusion is the entire last paragraph.

Standards and Benchmarks: 1D, 2C, 3A

Practice with Topics and Controlling Ideas

Read the following paragraph:

> Mrs. Smith became one of my favorite teachers when she went out of the way to help me when I was having trouble with math. Mrs. Smith would always come in early to help me and other students who had trouble understanding their multiplication and division problems. She would often think of activities using food, such as cookies or candy, to help us learn some difficult lesson. Whenever I had trouble understanding a new idea, she would go over it again but not embarrass me. I think I am doing well in math today because of the help Mrs. Smith gave me in the fifth grade.

Answer these questions about the paragraph.

1. What is the topic?

   _____

2. What is the controlling idea?

   _____

3. What are the three main supporting ideas?

   _____

   _____

   _____

   _____

   _____

   _____

4. Do you think the concluding sentence is a good one? Why?

   _____

   _____

   _____

Standards and Benchmarks: 1A

More Practice with Topics and Controlling Ideas

Before we write our own paragraph, let's practice some more with topics, controlling ideas, and supporting statements. Look at the following topic sentences. Each has one topic and one controlling idea. Underline the topic and circle the controlling idea. The topic of the first one is "smoking cigarettes." (Identifying the controlling idea should be easy for you now.) After you have done this for each topic sentence below, add two to three supporting statements for each one, beginning on the lines below and continuing on the back of the page.

1. Smoking cigarettes is harmful to your health.

   _____

2. Taking the train can save money.

   _____

3. Our state capitol building is one of the most beautiful in the country.

   _____

4. Sandra is a high school student who is very talented but quite shy.

   _____

5. The best tennis players need to be graceful.

   _____

6. Most students who want jobs must wait until they are 16.

   _____

7. Changing dollars into foreign currency can be confusing.

   _____

8. Developing computer skills will help you in high school.

   _____

9. Juan can eat more than anyone in our family, but he never gains weight.

   _____

10. Hiking in the woods is dangerous.

   _____

Standards and Benchmarks: 1A, 1D, 3A, 3J, 3K

More Practice with Topics and Controlling Ideas *(cont.)*

The topic sentence introduces the topic and controlling idea to your reader. Moreover, the controlling idea must clearly focus on a specific aspect or feeling. Look at the following:

A dog is a good pet.

The sentence is clear to a beginning reader. However, it is not really a developed sentence for a mature reader. It brings up questions that a better topic sentence would answer. *Why is a dog a good pet? Who is it good for? Are all dogs good pets?*

The personality of the cocker spaniel makes it an ideal pet for a young child.

Now the topic and controlling idea not only tell the reader what to expect, they also help the writer know how to develop the paragraph.

In each of the following groups of two, underline the one which is the *best* topic sentence. On the line which follows each paired group, explain your choice.

1. *The Sound of Music* is a delightful film.
2. The children in *The Sound of Music* make it a delightful film.

_____

3. New York is too crowded.
4. New York has many problems.

_____

5. Almost every large city has a K-Mart.
6. K-Mart is a good place to shop if you are on a budget.

_____

7. Many people still study Latin.
8. Studying Latin will also help you learn many difficult English words.

_____

9. Kodiak bears are among the largest types of bears and are found in Alaska.
10. Kodiak bears are dangerous for campers in Alaska.

_____

Standards and Benchmarks: 1A, 1B, 3A, 3J, 3K

More Practice with Topics and Controlling Ideas *(cont.)*

Read the following topic sentences. You will see that each has a weak topic or controlling idea or both. Rewrite each to make it more specific. The first one has been done for you.

1. Washington, D.C., is a beautiful city.

   <u>Washington, D.C., has some of the most beautiful monuments in the country.</u>

2. A school field trip is fun.

   _____

3. The movie was interesting.

   _____

4. Swimming is good for you.

   _____

5. Cats make the best pets.

   _____

6. Thanksgiving is a holiday.

   _____

7. My friend Beth should run for a school office.

   _____

8. Skateboarding is dangerous.

   _____

9. Many adults do not approve of skateboarding.

   _____

10. Some school rules seem unnecessary.

    _____

Standards and Benchmarks: 3A, 3J, 3K

Writing Complete Sentences

You may have been told that you have trouble writing complete sentences (*incomplete sentences are called **fragments***) or that you tend to write run-on sentences. Don't despair. Almost all student writers have trouble with these at some point in their education.

Fewer students have trouble with fragments than with run-ons. This page and the following two are for fragment problems. We will explore run-on problems in more depth in the later pages.

Fragments

If you are writing fragments, you might need to understand exactly how a simple sentence is composed.

A simple sentence consists of a <u>subject</u> and a <u>predicate</u>.

Here are four types of simple sentences.

❑ <u>Bob</u> <u>ran to the store</u>. (*a simple sentence with a single subject and a single predicate*)

❑ <u>Sandra and Maria</u> <u>share a locker at school</u>. (*a simple sentence with a compound subject and a single predicate*)

❑ <u>The children</u> <u>played and screamed on the playground</u>. (*a simple sentence with a single subject and a compound predicate*)

❑ <u>Joanna and Sarah</u> <u>walked around the campus and visited their friends</u>. (*a simple sentence with both a compound subject and a compound predicate*)

On the lines below, write your own simple sentences, following the patterns shown in the above sentences.

| Simple subject and simple predicate |

_____

| Compound subject and simple predicate |

_____

| Simple subject and compound predicate |

_____

| Compound subject and compound predicate |

_____

Standards and Benchmarks: 2C, 3A, 3J, 3K

Writing Complete Sentences *(cont.)*

Some writers run into trouble when they write a dependent clause and think it is a complete sentence.

- **Because I was late.**
- **Since no one was at home.**

Neither one of these is a complete sentence. Each must be connected to an independent clause in order to be complete.

The following are independent clauses:

- **Everyone was upset with me.**
- **The house was dark.**

We can put the independent clause and dependent clauses together:

> **Everyone was upset with me because I was late.**

> **The house was dark since no one was at home.**

A. Finding Dependent Clauses

Each of the following sentences has an independent clause and a dependent clause. Draw an oval around the independent clause and a box around the dependent clause.

Example: (I want Elizabeth as my locker partner) since she is so honest.

1. After Sam and Pete arrived, we began the meeting.

2. The teacher asked me to read since I have the loudest voice.

3. English and social studies are easy for me, although math is hard.

4. Unless you explain the problem carefully, no one will be able to understand it.

5. The ocean should be calm today unless there is a storm.

6. When the lightning began, the lifeguards made everyone come out of the water.

7. Before my sister was born, I was the only child in the house.

8. You will stay cool if you do not run around in the hot sun.

9. I like to sing, even though no one likes to hear me.

10. The house on the corner has the most beautiful garden because the owners work on it every weekend.

Standards and Benchmarks: 2C, 3A, 3I, 3K

Writing Complete Sentences (cont.)

B. Adding Independent Clauses

For each of the following dependent clauses, add an independent clause.

Example: **When the rain began**

| **When the rain began,** everyone ran inside. | Or, | Everyone ran inside **when the rain began.** |

1. when everyone made fun of him.

   _____

2. Unless the sun comes out,

   _____

3. Until someone turned on the lights,

   _____

4. before she took lessons.

   _____

5. because it was the wrong color.

   _____

6. After the game was over,

   _____

7. Even though I think skateboarding can be a safe sport,

   _____

8. As soon as I finish this assignment,

   _____

9. Although I dislike doing homework with my sister,

   _____

10. Although he is very smart,

    _____

11. If I never go to the mall again

    _____

12. Since it is such a nasty day,

    _____

13. If writing is more fun

    _____

14. even though we warned him.

    _____

15. If a dependent clause comes at the beginning of the sentence,

    _____

Standards and Benchmarks: 1A, 2C, 3A, 3I, 3J, 3K

Correcting Run-On Sentences

Most students write run-on sentences. It is actually easy to detect these and to correct them. What happens is that the writer strings two simple sentences together without a proper connection.

<u>Susan</u> wanted the job at the pet store <u>she</u> wasn't hired.

One way to improve this is to separate the sentences.

Susan wanted the job at the pet store. She wasn't hired.

However, a better way to improve this would be to combine the two sentences with a connecting word.

Susan wanted the job at the pet store, but ***she wasn't hired.***

Notice that the original two sentences are now connected with a *comma* and the word *but*. This is called a *compound sentence*.

Using compound sentences will really help improve your writing.

Here are the three most common compound sentence connectors:

, and		, but		, or

Again, notice that a comma precedes the words *and*, *but*, and *or* whenever they are used to connect *two whole sentences*.

Examples of run-on sentences corrected by using compound sentence connectors:

> **run-on:** My brother is a singer I am a dancer.
> **compound:** My brother is a singer, but I am a dancer.

> **run-on:** All my friends are coming to my party I am very excited.
> **compound:** All my friends are coming to my party, and I am very excited.

> **run-on:** Mary can take photography next semester she can take band.
> **compound:** Mary can take photography next semester, or she can take band.

Another type of sentence is the *complex sentence*. Actually, we were using these in the exercises on the previous page.

Here are some common complex sentence connectors:

- because
- since
- unless
- before
- after

- until
- if
- when
- whenever
- although

- as
- as soon as
- while
- though
- although

If you learn to use these connectors, you will cut down on the number of run-on sentences you write.

Standards and Benchmarks: 1A, 2C, 3A, 3I, 3J, 3K

Correcting Run-On Sentences *(cont.)*

Examples of run-on sentences corrected by using complex connectors:

> **run-on:** Maria doesn't like to cook she will help her mother on special occasions.
>
> **complex:** Maria doesn't like to cook, although she will help her mother on special occasions.

> **run-on:** The reporter wrote an article about the new teacher she interviewed him.
>
> **complex:** Before the reporter wrote an article about the new teacher, she interviewed him.

> **run-on:** I like to swim I don't like to surf.
>
> **complex:** Even though I like to swim, I don't like to surf.

You may know something special about complex sentences—the clauses can usually be switched from the back of the sentence to the front or from the front to the back.

I don't like to surf, even though I like to swim.

Sometimes they can be switched by changing a word or two.

Although Maria will help her mother on special occasions, Maria doesn't like to cook.

Sometimes a few words need to be changed if you switch clauses.

After she interviewed the new teacher, the reporter wrote an article about him.

Notice that whenever the dependent clause is first, a comma is needed between it and the independent clause. A dependent clause beginning with *although* or *even though* is always set off with commas, even when it comes at the end of a sentence.

> Even though the weatherman predicts rain, I intend to go to the Rose Bowl parade.
>
> I intend to go to the Rose Bowl parade, even though the weatherman predicts rain.

On the lines below write five correctly punctuated complex sentences of your own, using the connectors listed on the previous page.

_____

_____

_____

_____

_____

_____

Standards and Benchmarks: 1A, 2C, 3A, 3I, 3J, 3K

Correcting Run-On Sentences *(cont.)*

A. The following are run-on sentences. Correct them by adding a connecting word (and comma if needed). Make them either compound or complex as indicated in parentheses.

   1. I want to run she wants to walk. (*compound*)

   2. The car went over the cliff it was still burning. (*complex*)

   3. Martha came to my house she explained the homework to me. (*compound*)

   4. The class heard the last bell they ran quickly out of the room. (*complex*)

   5. Tom will go to a movie he can rent one. (*compound*)

   6. The parade float turned the corner the police stopped the traffic. (*complex*)

   7. Simon has made many friends he has only been here two months. (*complex*)

   8. The corn plants grew tall we took good care of them all winter. (*complex*)

   9. My neighbors will go on vacation to Costa Rica they will visit their relatives in Mexico. (*compound*)

   10. My parents hate my new shoes I love them! (*compound*)

Now for an added challenge, rewrite each of the sentences above, reversing the correction. For example, when you were asked to correct a run-on sentence above by making it into a compound sentence, this time make it complex.

   1. (*complex*) _____

   2. (*compound*) _____

   3. (*complex*) _____

   _____

   4. (*compound*) _____

   5. (*complex*) _____

   6. (*compound*) _____

   _____

   7. (*compound*) _____

   _____

   8. (*compound*) _____

   _____

   9. (*complex*) _____

   _____

   10. (*complex*) _____

   _____

Standards and Benchmarks: 1A, 1B, 2B, 2C, 3A, 3I, 3J, 3K

Correcting Run-On Sentences *(cont.)*

B. Revise the following paragraph by changing the simple sentences to compound or complex sentences where appropriate. *(Don't forget to use commas in the appropriate places.)* Use the lines underneath to rewrite the paragraph.

Mrs. Clay was a little girl in the 1960s. She celebrated her birthdays with her family. She loved parties. Some things about them bothered her. She always thought it was unfair to get too many presents. She knew many children in her community never got anything. Every passing year brought Mrs. Clay more concern. Now Mrs. Clay celebrates her birthdays at a local children's home. She gets some presents. She gives some presents. She thinks this is a meaningful celebration for her family. It shows them that others need their support. Her son, Michael, saves up a part of his allowance all year. He buys gifts for the homeless children. The Clay family is trying to persuade others to have their parties at the children's home. So far they have not been successful.

Standards and Benchmarks: 1B, 2B, 2C, 3A, 3I, 3J, 3K

Correcting Run-On Sentences *(cont.)*

C. Combining Sentences

Combine the following groups of sentences by using compound and complex connecting words. (*Remember to place your commas correctly.*) You should have one paragraph when you finish. Use the lines at the bottom of the page.

---

1. Sandra lived in New York City for ten years.
2. She moved to the country last March.

---

3. Sandra likes living in the country.
4. Sometimes she misses the excitement of the city.

---

5. There are no movies or plays in her little town.
6. She goes back to New York every three months.

---

7. She also visits some old friends.
8. Sandra's best friend, Adriana, would rather visit her.

---

9. Adriana likes the quiet in Sandra's town.
10. She often takes long walks in the woods.

---

11. Adriana likes seeing all the animals.
12. Horseback riding is one activity she never fails to do.

---

13. Sometimes Adriana thinks the wrong person moved to the country.
14. Sandra says she will never move back to New York City.

Brainstorming

Often a student is asked to write a paragraph or essay on a particular subject, and he or she cannot think of how to begin. This is true of professional writers, too. At times writers are assigned an article or even a book to write about a topic that they have never even thought much about. So how does a writer get started, whether he is a professional or a student who is asked to complete a school assignment?

One answer is *brainstorming*. On the following pages you will be shown some brainstorming techniques. These are great to use whenever you are thinking about what to write.

One of the basic advantages of these brainstorming techniques is that they enable you to come up with many aspects or sides of a given topic. It is important for writers to connect to an aspect of the topic that they are interested in. These techniques will work even when you think you have no interest in the topic at all.

Suppose the teacher gives you a choice about the topic of your next paragraph (or essay). You are to

1. Your Neighborhood

2. Table Manners

3. A Favorite School Subject

Many of us might agree there are probably few subjects that seem as boring as these. So now what? Actually, you have many options here. The task for you is to connect to one of them by brainstorming and then to formulate a controlling idea.

Free Writing	**The Five W Questions**	**Bubble Graph**
_____	Who? _____	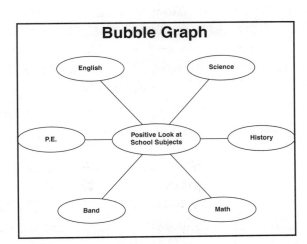
_____	What? _____	
_____	Where? _____	
_____	When? _____	
_____	Why? _____	

Standards and Benchmarks: 1A, 2A, 2B, 2C, 2D, 3A, 3B, 3C, 3D, 3E, 3F, 3G, 3H

Brainstorming *(cont.)*

Technique #1—**Free Writing**

In this technique you are to write for five or ten minutes on a subject without stopping. You are to put down whatever comes to your mind as fast as you can. Do not stop until the time is over. Try not to stop writing the entire time.

My Neighborhood

My neighborhood is not very interesting. There are about 14 houses on my block. There are only three houses with kids my age. The rest of the houses have old people in them or young adults who don't have any kids or very little kids. The people who live next door are very weird. We practically never see them. The husband and wife leave very early in the morning before I even get up. And they come home after dark. On the weekends they hardly ever come out of their house. Sometimes their newspaper stays out on the driveway all day. Once in a while I hear hammers banging in their closed garage. The people on the other side have two little girls. The parents are always yelling at the girls to pick up their toys. Sometimes we have to close our windows to get any peace. The family who lives right across the street is the strangest. The kids dress up for school every day. The two boys wear ties and sweaters—even when it is hot outside. The oldest child, a girl, always wears a skirt and blouse. Even on the weekend they are dressed up. Once I went over to ask the boy my age to play, but his mother said he wasn't allowed to play outside except in their backyard. She didn't ask me to come in, although I probably wouldn't have gone in anyway. What a crazy place I live in.

This student has written for ten minutes and was able to discuss three of the families who live on his street. He was most surprised to find that he has a lot more to write about his neighborhood than he thought. He actually has a very interesting neighborhood with many possible topics.

Let's list some of his possible topics and controlling ideas that he might be able to write an essay about.

1. The people next door could be spies.
2. My neighbors yell at their children so much that the girls are going to grow into unhappy teenagers.
3. The family across the street live as if they are in the 1950s.
4. There is no doubt that my family is the most normal in my neighborhood.
5. When I really think about it, my neighborhood is full of all sorts of interesting (strange, weird, unusual) people.

Standards and Benchmarks: 1A, 2A, 2B, 2D, 3A, 3B, 3C, 3D, 3E, 3F, 3G, 3H

Brainstorming *(cont.)*

Technique #1—**Free Writing** *(cont.)*

Beginning on the lines below and continuing on the back of this page if needed, write for five to ten minutes on your neighborhood. Concentrate on two or three of the families. Then formulate possible topics with controlling ideas.

_____

_____

_____

_____

_____

_____

_____

_____

_____

_____

_____

_____

_____

_____

_____

_____

_____

_____

_____

_____

_____

_____

Standards and Benchmarks: 2A, 2C, 3A, 3B, 3C, 3D, 3E, 3F, 3G, 3H, 3I, 3J, 3K

Brainstorming *(cont.)*

Technique #2—**The Five W Questions**

Your topic is the importance of table manners. What now? Right, you must develop a *controlling idea*. Try this brainstorming technique based on the five W questions that a newspaper article is supposed to cover: *Who? What? Where? When? Why?* Make up five W questions about the importance of table manners. Look at the following five examples.

1. **Who?**
   Who uses good table manners?

2. **What?**
   What is so important about good table manners?

3. **Where?**
   Where should a young person use good table manners?

4. **When?**
   When is an important time to be aware of your table manners?

5. **Why?**
   Why should anyone care about good table manners?

Here is how one student answered these questions:

1. **Anyone who wants to show that she is a sophisticated person should use good table manners.**

2. **Strangers often judge you by your table manners. They can decide what sort of a person you are and what your family has taught you by how you eat.**

3. **A young person should use good table manners when eating at a fancy restaurant on a special occasion like a birthday or holiday.**

4. **An important time to be aware of your table manners is when you are eating at your grandparent's house.**

5. **People should care about good table manners since no one likes to see someone else eating in a disgusting way.**

This student's answers might be used as the topic sentences for five separate paragraphs, actually. However, it would be better to look carefully at the responses and remember our wish to have a *clear topic* and *controlling idea* for each paragraph we write. Perhaps we can use the responses to the five W questions to form some really good topic sentences. It is worth the effort to craft excellent topic sentences, for then a good paragraph will be much easier to write.

Standards and Benchmarks: 1A, 2B, 2C, 3A, 3B, 3C, 3D, 3E, 3F, 3G, 3H, 3I, 3J, 3K

Brainstorming *(cont.)*

Technique #2—**The Five W Questions** *(cont.)*

So now what? One student used her first responses to the five W questions and came up with the following seven paragraph (or essay) topics with controlling ideas about table manners. Can you think of three more?

1. Almost all young people want to appear older, and having good table manners is one way to show you are mature.

2. Sometimes we are put into a situation where we must eat with people we have never met, and it is important to make a good impression.

3. If a young person enjoys eating at a fancy restaurant, she needs to show she can handle this special occasion by showing proper table manners so she can keep going out.

4. Grandparents often show their appreciation for the way their grandchildren act by giving presents, so good table manners are important when eating at your grandparents' house.

5. If a person hates to see another person be a slob while eating, she should be aware that she must practice proper table manners, too.

6. It is important to establish a good relationship with your boyfriend's parents, so use good table manners when eating at their house.

7. It is embarrassing to go out with your boyfriend and realize he is looking at you with a frown on his face while you are eating.

8. _____
_____
_____
_____

9. _____
_____
_____
_____

10. _____
_____
_____

Standards and Benchmarks: 1A, 2B, 2C, 3A, 3B, 3C, 3D, 3E, 3F, 3G, 3H, 3I, 3J, 3K

Brainstorming *(cont.)*

Technique #3—**Bubble Graph**

Here is a way of coming up with writing topics that you have probably used before. Let's look at one student's example and then see what controlling ideas she figures out from her graph.

Topic—A Favorite School Subject

```
        English                        Science


  P.E.          Positive Look at              History
                School Subjects


        Band                            Math
```

1. Math has turned out to be interesting after I learned how to work on word problems.

2. Marching band has turned out to be fun, especially the parades in which we've participated.

3. All my best friends are in English class, and we get together and have the best times studying.

4. My coach is very funny, and that's important the first period of the day.

5. Although I have no interest in old boring wars, I found out that I enjoy learning how people lived in ancient times.

6. It is fun to drive my science teacher crazy by continually messing up the experiments.

Try using the same idea with your subjects by concentrating on the positive elements in each class.

Standards and Benchmarks: 1A, 2B, 2C, 2D, 3A, 3B, 3C, 3D, 3E, 3F, 3G, 3H, 3I, 3J, 3K

Brainstorming *(cont.)*

Technique #4—**Looping**

Suppose the teacher gives you no subject at all and asks that you write an essay about whatever you want? Lucky you! Now you can use the most enjoyable technique of all. Just start writing about anything you want and write down the various thoughts which happen to pop into your mind. You don't even have to finish a whole thought if something else occurs that seems more interesting. The first subject? Whatever you are thinking right now. Just go.

I wish my mom wouldn't always yell at me about finishing my homework. My dad only yells at me when I make a stupid mistake on the soccer field. My sister never yells at me. In fact, she doesn't pay any attention to me. Why? I always try to do my best. My teacher is looking out the window. I wonder if she is bored. I am, too! Why do we always have to do these writing assignments? I know it is important to write well. Just like soccer. If I want to do better I have to practice. I also have to practice my guitar, but I like that. I have learned eight chords so far. I even wrote my own song called "Stopping by the Side of the Road." That's all I have so far with the words. I have the whole tune but only the title. Why do people stop by the side of the road? Flat tire? Pick someone up? To sleep? To get some fruit from the fruit stand? To look at the view? Last summer on vacation my family went up to the mountains, and my dad kept stopping the car to look at the view. Usually it was too foggy to see anything, which made all of us laugh. Even my sister was having a good time.

Now, pretend that you wrote the paragraph above. Look back over it and circle or loop any words that could be possible topics for your paragraph. After you have completed looping your choices, turn to the next page to compare your choices with those of another student. Notice how those choices were then used to form topics and controlling ideas.

Standards and Benchmarks: 1A, 2B, 2C, 2D, 3A, 3B, 3C, 3D, 3E, 3F, 3G, 3H, 3I, 3J, 3K

Brainstorming *(cont.)*

Technique #4—**Looping** *(cont.)*

After writing, this student went over his paragraph, looped possible topics and then wrote a controlling idea for each.

I wish my mom wouldn't always yell at me about finishing my (homework). My dad only yells at me when I make a stupid mistake on the (soccer) field. My (sister) never yells at me. In fact, she doesn't pay any attention to me. Why? I always try to do my best. My teacher is looking out the (window). I wonder if she is bored. I am, too! Why do we always have to do these writing assignments? I know it is important to write well. Just like soccer. If I want to do better I have to practice. I also have to practice my (guitar,) but I like that. I have learned eight chords so far. I even wrote my own song called "Stopping by the Side of the Road." That's all I have so far with the words. I have the whole tune but only the title. Why do people stop by the side of the road? (Flat tire?) (Pick someone up?) To sleep? To get some fruit from the fruit stand? To look at the view? Last summer on vacation my (family) went up to the (mountains,) and my dad kept stopping the car to look at the view. Usually it was too foggy to see anything, which made all of us laugh. Even my sister was having a good time.

1. **homework**—Teachers should realize that students do have a life outside of school and not assign so much homework.
2. **soccer**—I am the best forward on my soccer team now that we have a coach who knows what he is doing.
3. **sister**—My sister is only three years older than I am, yet she acts like she is on a special planet because she was born first.
4. **window**—Great ideas can come to people if they really see what is happening right outside their window.
5. **guitar**—My guitar is my most valuable possession because I would rather be playing that than doing anything else.
6. **flat tire**—Fixing a flat tire is a very strenuous activity.
7. **pick someone up**—It is too bad it is dangerous to pick up a hitchhiker because you could really meet some interesting people that way.
8. **family**—There are actually times when my family has a good time together.
9. **mountains**—I like playing outside all year long, so it would be difficult to live in the mountains.

Standards and Benchmarks: 1A, 2B, 2C, 2D, 3A, 3B, 3C, 3D, 3E, 3F, 3G, 3H, 3I, 3J, 3K

Brainstorming *(cont.)*

Now you try the looping technique.

Just start writing.

_____

_____

_____

_____

_____

_____

_____

_____

_____

_____

_____

_____

Now loop some likely words in your paragraph above and then formulate some topics with controlling ideas:

1. _____

2. _____

3. _____

4. _____

5. _____

6. _____

7. _____

8. _____

9. _____

10. _____

Standards and Benchmarks: 2B, 2C, 3A, 3B, 3C, 3D, 3E, 3F, 3G, 3H, 3I, 3J, 3K

Paragraph Model

Automobiles are expensive to own. After buying a car you have to have money for insurance that the law says you must have in case of an accident. Cars, even new ones, need occasional costly repairs. Even if you drive carefully, you will sometimes make mistakes and might get a ticket, which you must pay for or your license will be taken away. Even if you never get in an accident or get a ticket, you have to fill the car with gas, and prices are at an all-time high.

- Why is the topic sentence a good one? _____
- Do the supporting sentences explain the controlling idea?_____
- Are all the sentences related? _____
- Underline your choice of the following for a concluding sentence to this paragraph.

    1. Owning a car will cost the owner plenty of money.

    2. Also, you could get in trouble driving without a license.

    3. Commercials on television tell you that you must have insurance.

- Why didn't you pick either of the other two? _____

Choose one of the following topics and write a clear expository paragraph.

1. fast-food restaurants   4. learning a language

2. horror movies   5. a music group

3. any sport   6. any topic that you have an idea or attitude about

_____

_____

_____

_____

_____

_____

_____

_____

Standards and Benchmarks: 1B, 1D, 2B, 2C, 3A, 3B, 3C, 3D, 3E, 3F, 3G, 3H, 3I, 3J, 3K

Peer Checklist
for Your Paragraph

When you have finished your paragraph and have reread it to correct any obvious mistakes, give it to a classmate to read. The reader is to read the paragraph carefully at least twice before answering the following.

Writer: _____

Reader: _____

Date: _____

1. What is the topic of the paragraph?

   _____

2. What is the controlling idea?

   _____

3. Do you feel it is an acceptable topic sentence? Explain why you think it is clear and focused or tell what the problem is.

   _____

   _____

   _____

4. Is the paragraph unified? (Do all the sentences support the controlling idea?) Point out any problems.

   _____

   _____

5. Which of the supporting sentences do you feel is the most interesting?

   _____

6. Tell the writer what he or she has done well.

   _____

   _____

   _____

Return this checklist and paragraph to the writer.

The Positive Side of Being in Student Government

The following essay model will be referred to in this section.

People looking for a way to be involved in school activities might consider student government. Almost all people who have ever been in student government will agree that it was a worthwhile experience on many levels—whether they enjoy being the center of attention, like to be in control, or think it will look good on their resumés. Holding a school office will bring many rewards.

Some people enjoy being in the middle of school activities. They think others will look up to them and seek their company. They like to read the announcements over the P.A. system so others will think they are special. Officers in student government can be part of the activities every day and be seen by many people. They think that others will ask their advice and approval. Student officers don't have to think about where they will go during lunch or after school. Wherever they are, that's where the action is.

Some people who want to be student officers like to feel in command. They don't like being followers. They want to be part of activities where they can state their views and others will listen. They like to lead people and let others see them being leaders. For example, they like being on stage during assemblies or meeting all the new students as they come to register. These people also like to have the last word. They like to decide what activities to have during "Hawaiian" week or the eighth-grade dance.

Another group joins student government because it will look good when they get to high school or apply for a first job. They understand that administrators want students with experience. Many feel that advisors will accept their application if it says they were in student government in middle school. When applying for work, student officers may feel that bosses will consider them before anyone else. They think employers will understand that they have had experience in handling problems. Also, they will see this applicant as a leader, possibly one to consider for a managerial position.

It is probably not possible to find a more worthwhile activity in school than student government. It gives the officers many ways to improve. Whether they want to be in the center of what is going on, be in charge of activities, or find ways of improving their applications at the end of a middle school career, student government will help them achieve their goals.

Standards and Benchmarks: 1A, 1B, 1D, 2C, 3A, 3I, 3J, 3K

The Positive Side of Being in Student Government *(cont.)*

Answer these questions about the essay on student government found on page 47.

1. In the first paragraph what is the opinion or attitude? Where is this found?

   _____

   _____

   _____

2. What is the controlling idea in paragraph two? paragraph three? paragraph four?

   _____

   _____

   _____

   _____

3. How does the last paragraph sum up the essay?

   _____

   _____

4. Can you think of other reasons for being a part of student government?

   _____

   _____

5. Come up with a list of reasons for not joining student government.

   _____

   _____

   _____

   _____

6. Suppose you must write an essay about why joining student government is a poor idea. Compose a thesis statement.

   _____

   _____

   _____

Standards and Benchmarks: 1A, 1D, 2C, 3I, 3J, 3K

Thesis Statements

An expository essay, like the paragraph, is controlled by one central idea. In an essay this controlling idea is called the *thesis statement*. In our model essay on page 47, the thesis statement is *Holding a school office will bring you many rewards.* It is a complete sentence restating the topic—*school office*—and a controlling idea—*bring many rewards.*

A thesis statement must be stated in a complete sentence, which is usually found in the last sentence in the introduction.

"My dad's love of swimming" is not a complete sentence. There is a topic here but no controlling idea.

- **If my dad hadn't loved swimming as a teenager, he might not have developed into a landscape designer.**

Now we have a topic and a controlling idea. The writer's job now is to explain how her father's love of swimming made him choose landscape designing as his occupation.

A thesis statement expresses an attitude or opinion much like the topic sentence. The difference is that it will cover a larger topic, which will take several paragraphs to prove. In our model essay on being in student government, the only real attitude or opinion is found in the thesis—*bring many rewards.* The first sentence states a fact. The middle sentence contains information. Only the final sentence states an opinion. Always make sure your thesis statement has a topic and a controlling idea.

- **I am going to discuss the camera.**

Here, once again, we have a topic, but no idea how it will be developed. (Also, if you are going to write an essay about the camera, you do not have to include *I am going to discuss . . . . We* already understand this—we have your essay!)

Let's add a controlling idea to our thesis statement.

- **A camera with a zoom lens will make your pictures more exciting.**

Notice that this thesis statement contains a clearly worded opinion— *"Your pictures will be more exciting (with a zoom lens)."*

Standards and Benchmarks: 1A, 1D, 2C, 3A, 3I, 3J, 3K

Thesis Statements *(cont.)*

Would the following make a better opening sentence or a thesis statement?

Air conditioning is used in many schools today.

This sentence has a topic, but the controlling idea is a fact. There is nothing to prove. It should *not be used* as a thesis statement. How does the writer continue after using only a fact as the thesis statement? With more facts, of course, but that is not really well-developed expository writing.

- **A school with air conditioning makes it easier for students to concentrate.**

Now we have an arguable statement. Why is it arguable? It is arguable since another person could have a different idea about the topic and try to prove it.

How could another student argue an opposite point? How about these thesis statements?

- **Students do not need air conditioning since their parents did as well in school without it.**

- **Air conditioning creates allergies in students who never had them before.**

- **Air conditioning in school never seems to work correctly since it is either too hot or too cold.**

A thesis statement should be just **one opinion or attitude** *about one topic.* If there are two or more ideas, the essay could be difficult to write. Suppose our model essay ended the introduction with this thesis statement:

- *Holding a school office will bring a person many rewards, and he or she should also understand the importance of leading people.*

The problem here is there are **two controlling ideas that need two separate essays** to adequately discuss.

Here is another one:

- *Visiting a new city is educational, and the area around Washington, D.C., is beautiful.*

There are two topics and two controlling ideas here. Which one will the writer focus on? Such a thesis statement will confuse both writer and reader.

- *The area around Washington, D.C., has great natural beauty.*

Now this would be arguable in an essay. The writer would clearly know what he must prove. Furthermore, the reader would know what to expect the writer to prove.

Standards and Benchmarks: 1A, 1B, 1D, 2C, 3A, 3I, 3J, 3K

Thesis Statements *(cont.)*

Activitiy

For each confusing thesis statement, write a correction or improved statement by focusing on one controlling idea.

1. Getting an after-school job can help you pay for school expenses, and it can cause you to stay up too late at night to finish your homework.

   _____

   _____

   _____

2. If I had an opportunity to go anywhere in the world, I would choose to see Italy, or perhaps I would go just visit the northern part of my state.

   _____

   _____

   _____

3. The most beautiful season is winter when the snow makes the whole city clean and white, but I like summer when there is no school.

   _____

   _____

   _____

4. Sports participation is an important part of growing up, and many students like to also just participate in whatever other activity interests them.

   _____

   _____

   _____

5. Wherever you find drugs being used, you also will find crime, and many adults think teens don't understand or care how terrible drug addiction is.

   _____

   _____

   _____

6. Taking care of older family members who need help is a responsibility of everyone, and I well remember how my grandmother told me fascinating stories of her childhood.

   _____

   _____

   _____

Thesis Statements (cont.)

Reproduce these rules for the bulletin board and one copy for each student.

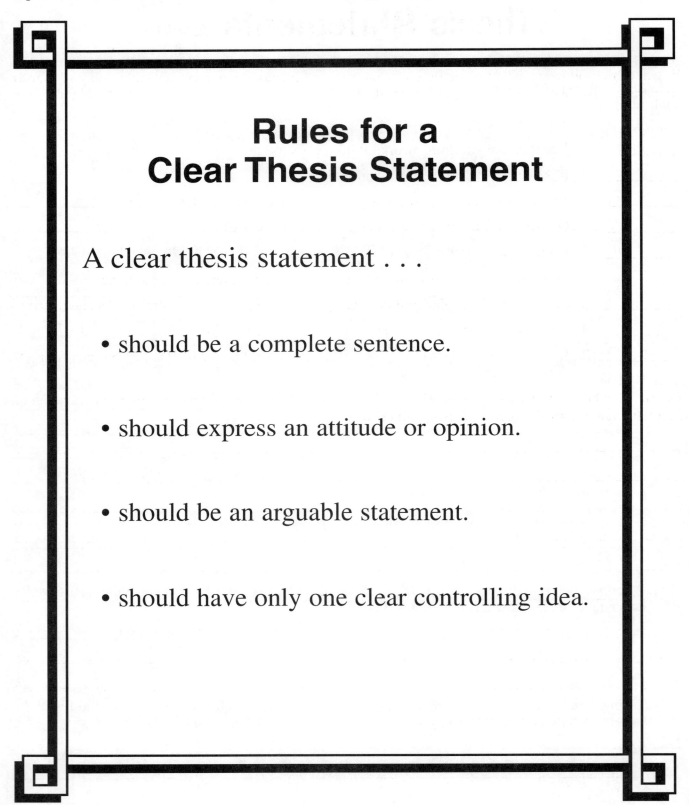

Rules for a
Clear Thesis Statement

A clear thesis statement . . .

- should be a complete sentence.

- should express an attitude or opinion.

- should be an arguable statement.

- should have only one clear controlling idea.

Standards and Benchmarks: 2C, 3A, 3I, 3J, 3K

Thesis Statements *(cont.)*

Which of the following are arguable thesis statements which could be proved in a short essay of four to six paragraphs? Write either *yes* or *no* in the blank.

_____ 1. The fun of a birthday party.

_____ 2. I think there are many ways of thinking about school.

_____ 3. It is healthier to drink water than soda.

_____ 4. The law says everyone must stay in school until the age of 16.

_____ 5. Our school cafeteria needs to have vegetarian choices.

_____ 6. I would like to tell you about my room.

_____ 7. Most people will find swimming a more beneficial exercise than jogging.

_____ 8. Being in a school play will decrease your fear of performing in front of an audience.

_____ 9. The Academy Awards ceremony takes place in Los Angeles.

_____ 10. Planting trees in your front yard will improve the look of your home, but don't forget about painting the house, too.

On the lines below, write what you think would be improved versions of the statements above which you felt were not good, arguable thesis statements.

_____

_____

_____

_____

_____

_____

_____

_____

_____

_____

_____

_____

Standards and Benchmarks: 1B, 2C, 3A, 3I, 3J, 3K

Revising Thesis Statements

None of the following is a thesis statement. Revise each one so it has a clear topic and a controlling idea that can be proved in a short essay. The first one shows you one possible answer.

1. I am going to tell you why I decided to take piano lessons.
   My lifelong love of music led me to ask my parents for piano lessons.

2. It is difficult to learn a foreign language. _____

3. There are not enough ice-skating rinks in our city, and there are not enough parks to play basketball or soccer.

4. There are many advantages to living in an apartment.

5. The Internet. _____

6. I think kindness to animals is a good character trait, and today much cruelty is shown by people who are not vegetarians or by racing dogs and horses.

7. I have my own reasons for preparing to go to college.

8. Many of today's movies are rated to help parents decide whether to take their children to see them.

9. Los Angeles, California, has many freeways filled with cars and trucks.

10. Some parents do not approve of the music listened to by their children.

The Introduction

Where should the thesis statement be placed in your introductory paragraph? Although there is no single place that it must be, the most common is in *the last sentence of the first paragraph.* We will practice putting the thesis statement at the end of the introduction paragraph.

Look at the following model:

> Trees can change the look of a neighborhood. Trees provide shade, windbreaks, and homes for singing birds. Every homeowner should be required to plant at least one tree in the front of the house.

Find the topic and controlling idea in the last sentence.

Topic—*every homeowner*

Controlling idea—*should be required to plant a tree.*

- What else do you notice about the paragraph? The first sentence is a statement that is a fact. No one can disagree that trees change the look of a neighborhood. Notice there is no opinion here. It does not say that a tree makes a neighborhood look better or worse.

- The second sentence shows ways the first sentence is true. Again, it is not an opinion. These are facts which help show why the first sentence is a fact.

- The third, or thesis sentence, states the opinion. The writer's task is to prove that a homeowner should be required to plant trees. Here is our controlling idea.

In an essay, the entire first paragraph sets up the topic and controlling idea. **The thesis statement (topic and controlling idea) is placed at the end of the first paragraph so it is fresh in the reader's mind as the writer starts his proof in the developmental or body paragraphs.**

Introductory Paragraph Diagram

Sentence One . . . .

Sentence Two . . . .

Sentence Three . . . .

Sentence Four . . . .

Thesis Statement . . . .

Standards and Benchmarks: 1A, 1B, 2C, 3A, 3I, 3J, 3K

The Introduction *(cont.)*

Try writing a thesis statement at the end of each of these paragraphs.

1. Most children enjoy owning a dog. Dogs provide many opportunities for a child to mature. Dogs require care, provide love, and are always there to keep the child company.

   _____

   _____

   _____

2. Police officers are important members of their community. They protect citizens from harm. They are helpful to people who are suffering. When we see a police officer, it reminds us to respect the law.

   _____

   _____

   _____

Notice that in each paragraph the first sentence stated a fact. The second (and third and fourth) sentences expressed ways the first sentences could be discussed. The thesis that you write should give an opinion about the sentences that came before it.

Try one more.

3. Much of the population eats at a restaurant at least once a week. Restaurants save time for busy parents who don't always have time to make their family a weekday meal. Restaurants provide a break for busy mothers who work all day. Many people think of restaurants as part of their entertainment.

   _____

   _____

   _____

   Which one of the three is your best thesis statement? Why?

   _____

   _____

   _____

Share your best one with a classmate while you read theirs.

The Introduction *(cont.)*

Expository writing must prove the attitude or opinion the writer states, whether it is just a paragraph, an essay, or a 500-page book. Most expository writing is nonfiction and can therefore be compared to how a trial is conducted, since the law often deals with facts. However, facts may be dealt with in different ways, depending on which side of the case is important to a participant. A lawyer must prove his case to the jury. The writer must prove his statement to the reader. A lawyer argues only one side of the case (his or her attitude or opinion). The writer states one view of a topic and attempts to prove it. A lawyer will not usually bring up facts that could help the opposing lawyer's case. Likewise, a writer uses only proof that will help his or her case.

Suppose you are a lawyer and your client is a student accused of jaywalking on a busy street. Which of these would you use to defend your client?

1. **The crosswalk was not clearly marked.**

2. **The student had been kept late after school and felt that he did not have time to walk to the corner.**

3. **The student frequently was seen crossing in the middle of the block.**

4. **On the day the student was given a jaywalking ticket, he had a sore foot and he was needed at home to help his mother take care of his baby sister.**

5. **He was just one of eight students who crossed in the middle of the block.**

Let's assume that all five statements are true about your client. However, you would probably only use one, two, and four since these are the ones that would help the jaywalker. Numbers three and five could be used to show the student to be careless and perhaps simply a weak person who followed the crowd.

When nonfiction writing is called *factual*, we must remember that there are many ways of looking at facts. Can you see why a writer of expository writing may be compared to a lawyer?

Standards and Benchmarks: 1A, 1B, 1D

The Introduction *(cont.)*

Read the following paragraph and answer the question that follows.

> A continent is a great area of land. There are seven continents in the world. They are Asia, Africa, North America, South America, Europe, and Australia. Some people also consider Antarctica as a continent.

What fact does the first sentence state that cannot be argued? What is arguable in the paragraph? Is this an expository paragraph? Why?

_____

_____

_____

If you answered the next-to-last question by saying that there is no arguable statement, you are correct. A lawyer or writer could not really argue about any of the statements in this paragraph. Suppose the last sentence was, *Although many people consider Antarctica as a separate continent, it should never be included in the list.* Is this now an arguable statement that could be proven with facts? The answer is, of course, yes. Notice that the previous sentence says "could" be proven. This means another person could attempt to explain why Antarctica should be considered a continent.

Let's read another paragraph about the continents, using some of the same information:

> A continent is a great area of land. Each continent, like Asia or Europe, has many beautiful natural landmarks. Of all continents, however, North America has the most varied natural formations.

This is better since it has an arguable thesis sentence. However, it does not help the writer to know what should come next.

Read this paragraph:

> North America has some beautiful natural landmarks which people from all over the world enjoy visiting. The Grand Canyon is probably the most famous with its breathtaking views of mile-deep valleys. Yosemite has incredible waterfalls. The Cascade Mountains of Canada are full of varied animal life. Visiting the natural sights of these three areas is a must for all travelers.

- This paragraph is better since it has unity.
- It begins by stating a fact about North America.
- No time is wasted by talking about the other continents.
- The three central sentences limit the topic to three areas. Each of these three sentences gives the writer some area to concentrate on in the paragraphs to come.
- Finally, the thesis sentence states an opinion that the writer can prove in the essay.

Standards and Benchmarks: 1A, 1B, 1C, 1D, 1E, 2A, 2B, 2C, 3A, 3I, 3J, 3K

Writing Introductory Paragraphs

Let's try to write our own introductory paragraphs. Below you will find several facts which could be used to open an essay. Your job is to write at least two more sentences for each. *The middle sentence(s) should give some examples* that can be used to support the first sentence. *The last sentence,* we know, *must state an opinion or attitude.* (You can change the sentences below if they do not serve your paragraph well.)

1. All schools can use improvement, and ours is no different.

2. Almost all students look forward to summer vacation.

3. Eating continuously at fast-food restaurants can cause problems.

4. Computer training is important for the future.

Use the space below to write one introductory paragraph.

_____

_____

_____

_____

_____

_____

_____

_____

_____

_____

_____

_____

Share your paragraph with a classmate. Your classmate will fill out the comment sheet on page 60 and attach it to your paragraph.

Standards and Benchmarks: 1A, 1D, 2C, 3A, 3I, 3J, 3K

Writing Introductory Paragraphs *(cont.)*

Student Comments

Answer these questions about the paragraph you read. Read the paragraph at least twice. Write your comments on this sheet and then attach it to the paragraph.

1. Was there a fact stated in the first sentence that cannot be argued? What is it?

   _____

   _____

2. What has the writer made you think he or she will discuss in the developmental paragraphs?

   _____

   _____

3. What is the topic? What is the controlling idea?

   _____

   _____

4. Make a positive comment about this paragraph.

   _____

   _____

5. What do you think will be the writer's topic sentence for the first body paragraph? Write a possibility.

   _____

   _____

6. What do you think will be the writer's topic sentence for the second body paragraph? Write a possibility.

   _____

   _____

7. Based on the introduction, do you think there will be a third body paragraph? Explain.

   _____

   _____

Developmental Paragraphs

Developmental or body paragraphs usually number from two to four in most student essays. They provide explanation, illustration, discussion, or proof of the thesis statement.

Each developmental paragraph discusses one aspect of the main topic. If you write about some of the ways trees have an impact on a neighborhood street, each paragraph should discuss one of those ways or functions.

Each developmental or body paragraph should echo or refer to the thesis statement. If your thesis statement says "every homeowner should plant trees," then each controlling idea should have something to do with the reason every homeowner should plant a tree.

The developmental paragraphs should flow. The flow of thoughts from one paragraph should flow into the next. This can be done through *transitions*, which will be discussed in the following units.

One way to form developmental paragraphs is to ask yourself a question about your thesis.

Thesis—*Watching TV is a waste of time.*

Question—Why is watching TV a waste of time?

Answers

1. Watching TV takes attention away from your schoolwork.
2. When you are watching TV, you aren't doing the household jobs you promised to do.
3. Watching TV keeps you from talking to your family and friends.

Thesis—*My brothers are more alike than they are different.*

Question—How are my brothers alike?

Answers

1. They have the same hair and eye color.
2. Neither of them gets angry easily.
3. Soccer is their favorite sport.

Standards and Benchmarks: 1A, 1B, 1C, 1D, 2A, 2C, 3I, 3J, 3K

Developmental Paragraphs *(cont.)*

Fill in the charts using two of the revised sentences you wrote on page 54. For this exercise, you will use them as thesis statements.

A. Thesis: _____

_____

Question: _____

_____

Answers

   1. _____

_____

   2. _____

_____

   3. _____

_____

B. Thesis: _____

_____

Question: _____

_____

Answers

   1. _____

_____

   2. _____

_____

   3. _____

_____

Stealing Your Time

(The following essay model will be referred to in this section.)

Most people have at least one television in their homes. Many have a set in every room. Many problems are connected with watching too much TV. It takes attention away from your schoolwork. When you are watching TV, you easily forget about the tasks you promised to do. Also, it can keep you from communicating with your family and friends. Basically, watching TV is a waste of valuable time.

One of the ways TV wastes time is that it steals the opportunity to do the best job on your schoolwork. Often you know there is work to complete. However, instead of spending the required time, you will turn on the TV. With the program taking your full attention, it is easy to forget about your assignment. By the time you remember the assignment, it is time to go to bed. So you hurry through the schoolwork, not to do a good job but just to get it done. The television has taken away your opportunity to better understand that school subject.

A second way TV can take away valuable time is by leading you to put off chores you promised to do. Suppose a parent has asked you to fix dinner so she could run to the store to get you supplies for your science project. However, you decide to see what is on TV. You find something to watch, although you probably wouldn't watch it if you had an opportunity to play with your best friend. You hear your mother's car parking in front of your house. Suddenly, you realize what you failed to do. Now your mother is angry with you. However, what is worse is that you cannot be depended on to keep your promise. TV has taken more than time away from you this time.

Another, and often the worst, way TV can waste valuable time is by taking away an opportunity for you to communicate with people around you. The kind of conversation that goes on between people watching TV is very superficial. There is not much thinking going on since the main part of the attention is focused on the "box." Often people who are watching TV in the same room are really not connected at all. They are off in their own world. Television takes away the chance for you to forge meaningful relationships. Many persons might say that there are positive aspects to watching TV. However, there are many more disadvantages to spending most of your free time in front of "the tube." Television steals time from schoolwork, chores, and the opportunity to connect to live people. If TV is hurting you, then you are spending too much time watching it.

Standards and Benchmarks: 1A, 1D, 2C, 3A, 3I, 3J, 3K

Stealing Your Time (cont.)

Answer the following questions about the TV essay on page 63.

1. What is the main topic of the essay? What is the controlling idea? Copy the topic sentence.

_____

_____

_____

2. What is the controlling idea for each of the subtopics?

_____

_____

_____

_____

_____

3. Does the writer prove her point? Do you agree or disagree? Explain.

_____

_____

_____

4. Write two or three other thesis statements for an expository essay about watching TV.

_____

_____

_____

_____

_____

_____

_____

_____

Standards and Benchmarks: 1A, 1B, 1D, 2B, 2C, 3A, 3I, 3J, 3K

Conclusions

The introduction opens the essay, and the conclusion wraps up the discussion, bringing it to a logical end. But the conclusion is often difficult to write. What do you say? Although what you say always depends on what the essay is about, there are some standard rules about any conclusion.

- **The conclusion can restate the main points.** Look at the controlling ideas in each of the paragraphs.
- **The conclusion can restate the thesis.** It is important to make sure your reader is again reminded of your main idea.
- **The conclusion should not bring up a new topic.** The conclusion is not the place to bring up a completely new controlling idea that needs support. If you want to give some more support to your topic, write another developmental (*body*) paragraph, using the back of this page.

An essay about natural landmarks in North America might conclude like this:

> There are many beautiful places to visit in North America. If you were to visit all of them, it would take you a lifetime. If you had time to visit only three, the Grand Canyon, Yosemite, and the Cascade Mountains would be excellent choices. For any visitor who cares for nature, these three areas show the many varied ways this continent is blessed with great wonders.

Following is a brief outline of an essay. There is a thesis statement followed by three supporting ideas. Try to write a concluding paragraph.

Thesis Statement

> The food in San Francisco is unusual and surprising for the people who visit this fascinating city.

Support

1. Chinese cuisine found in the Chinatown area is often considered the best in the United States.

2. The restaurants in the Italian section of North Beach often specialize in food from one small section of Italy.

3. The area of Fisherman's Wharf has developed dishes that originated in this city.

Concluding Paragraph

_____

_____

_____

_____

_____

Standards and Benchmarks: 1A, 1B, 1C, 1F, 2B, 2C, 3A, 3I, 3J, 3K

Writing a Trial Essay

You may not feel ready to write an essay of your own. However, you have two models to follow—"The Positive Side of Being in School Government" and "Stealing Your Time" (pages 47 and 63). Remember that learning to write well requires us to try and to be willing to learn from mistakes.

Below are some topics. Choose one and fill in the chart. Then use the information you gathered to write an essay on another sheet of paper.

Possible topics. Use the same exercise you practiced on pages 61 and 62 (Developmental Paragraphs). Develop your chart into an essay. Use the model essays as a guide.

1. a brother or sister
2. taking a trip to a new place
3. playing on a sports team
4. your favorite type of music
5. your favorite or least favorite school subject
6. your choice of any topic about which you have an idea or attitude

Thesis Statement:

_____

_____

_____

Question:

_____

_____

_____

Supporting Statements:

1. _____

_____

2. _____

_____

3. _____

_____

Standards and Benchmarks: 1D, 2C, 3A, 3I, 3J, 3K

Peer Checklist for Your Trial Essay

When you have finished your essay and have reread it to correct obvious mistakes, give it to a classmate to read. The classmate is to read the essay carefully at least twice before answering the following.

Writer: _____

Reader: _____

Date: _____

1. What are the topic and controlling idea of the essay?

   _____

   _____

2. Do you have any suggestions about the introduction and/or thesis statement?

   _____

   _____

3. Does the first developmental (body) paragraph support the thesis? Any suggestions?

   _____

   _____

4. Does the second (and third) developmental paragraph support the thesis? Any suggestions?

   _____

   _____

5. Do you have any suggestions about the conclusion?

   _____

   _____

6. What is the best part of the essay?

   _____

   _____

7. Which part of the essay needs the most improvement? Explain why.

   _____

   _____

Restaurants Define San Francisco

(The following examples essay model will be referred to in this section.)

San Francisco has hundreds of restaurants. One unique characteristic of this city's restaurants is that they are found in their own special areas. Chinatown is famous for its Chinese cuisine. Italian restaurants can be found in the North Beach area. Down at Fisherman's Wharf seafood is the specialty. The restaurant locations in the special neighborhoods of San Francisco make the experience of dining very special.

The food of Chinatown is made even more special by the wonderful area where a visitor finds the restaurants. Most of the people who eat at the restaurants are Chinese-Americans. They demand true Chinese cooking, and the restaurants provide fresh abalone or shark-fin soup. You will find hundreds of Chinese cakes and pastries—not just fortune cookies. After eating you can visit a Chinese museum or Buddhist temple right next door. The reason for this special area that looks like an Asian city is that more Chinese live in San Francisco's Chinatown than anyplace else outside of China.

North Beach is home to many of the wonderful Italian restaurants that are part of San Francisco history. First, to work up an appetite, try walking down Lombard Street, "the crookedest street in the world." Then after climbing Telegraph Hill, it is time for some great Italian food. Before the city had its famous earthquakes and fire in 1906, there were several Italian restaurants. During the last 90 years, however, Italians have opened new places on every corner of North Beach, specializing in food from particular areas of Italy. Tired of spaghetti? Then at noon try calzone, and by six or seven you'll be ready for some spinach canneloni. Before the chefs and waiters of these restaurants left their native Italy, they learned everything about authentic cooking. After leaving a restaurant, customers might even be lucky enough to hear an Italian song from a nearby opera school.

Ride the cable car to Fisherman's Wharf to have your choice of close to a hundred places to eat. They range from carts which sell seafood cocktails to elaborate restaurants with every type of fish imaginable. Don't leave without trying some ahi tuna, octopus, or eel. All these restaurants offer the very freshest fish. Much of it probably came out of the same bay that you are viewing from your table. Tied up along the wharf you can see the very boats that caught your fish. All these details make a visit to Fisherman's Wharf a special occasion. But don't be surprised that what you might remember most is the unique combination of smells of the fish, bay, and great sourdough French bread.

San Francisco's unique areas provide some of the most wonderfully delicious and unusual food in the world. What is most distinctive is the area where you find the restaurants. Chinese temples next to the restaurants of Chinatown, opera schools across the street from an Italian eatery, and fishing boats next to your table at Fisherman's Wharf—the locations of restaurants in San Francisco have no equal.

Standards and Benchmarks: 1A, 1B, 1C, 1D, 2C, 3A, 3I, 3J, 3K

Restaurants Define San Francisco *(cont.)*

Answer these questions about the essay "Restaurants Define San Francisco."

1. What is the topic?

_____

_____

_____

_____

2. What is the controlling idea? Write out the thesis statement, putting quotation marks around it.

_____

_____

_____

3. What are the three types of food used to develop the topic?

_____

_____

_____

4. How does each area of San Francisco help the visitor appreciate the food?

_____

_____

_____

5. What should you do in San Francisco before you try some Italian food? Why?

_____

_____

_____

6. At Fisherman's Wharf what kind of unusual fish might you try?

_____

_____

_____

Standards and Benchmarks: 1A, 1B, 1C, 1D, 2C, 3A, 3I, 3J, 3K

Restaurants Define San Francisco (cont.)

Answer these questions about the essay "Restaurants Define San Francisco."

7. What do the boats docked near the restaurants have to do with the food you might eat?

_____

_____

_____

8. What unusual fact does the writer use at the end of the paragraph concerning what you might most remember about Fisherman's Wharf?

_____

_____

_____

9. Why might the writer have waited until the end of the essay to give you this information about Fisherman's Wharf?

_____

_____

_____

10. If a visitor to San Francisco were telling about his visit to Chinatown, which piece of information might be most interesting to the listener?

_____

_____

_____

11. Where is this information placed in the paragraph?

_____

_____

_____

12. Do you think the writer proved his topic about the areas of San Francisco? Explain.

_____

_____

_____

The Examples Paragraph

Before we progress to writing an examples essay, let's begin with the examples paragraph. An examples paragraph *will state the topic and controlling idea in the first sentence.* There will be examples to support the topic in the middle sentences. The last sentence of the paragraph will conclude the short discussion. We will start looking at the examples paragraph, and after we feel comfortable we will move on to the examples essay.

> Going to surf camp is expensive. First, you have to pay for the instruction from qualified teachers who have lifesaving experience. Second, there is the equipment. You'll need a surfboard, of course, but also a wet suit and ocean shoes. Last, you will need transportation to the ocean which, if you live miles from the water, will require air or train tickets. Just learning to surf might seem easy, but getting ready to learn will cost a great deal of money.

Let's analyze the paragraph.

- **Topic**—*surf camp*
- **Controlling Idea**—*is expensive*
- **Support**—*cost of instruction, cost of surfboard, wet suit, transportation*
- **Conclusion**—*a simple-looking activity can cost plenty*

Can this be developed into an essay? Yes, but you will have to do some more thinking. You'll want to give plenty of statistics on what these different items cost.

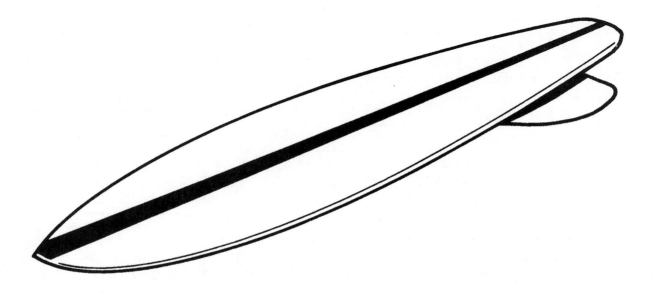

Standards and Benchmarks: 1A, 1D, 1E

The Examples Paragraph *(cont.)*

We have practiced quite a bit with topic sentences and controlling ideas, so let's turn our attention to the support. Support in expository writing *must be specific enough to prove your controlling idea.*

Look at this sentence.

> My neighborhood is noisy.

Now that you have written that your neighborhood is noisy, you must support it with examples that prove your case. Which of these following sentences will help you prove it? Write the topic sentence first and then add your choices of the sentences below. Add them in the order that you think would be best to make an effective paragraph.

1. One family has three teenagers, and each has a boombox blaring whenever they are home.

2. There are almost 30 houses on our streets.

3. The garbage collectors come every Thursday.

4. My next-door neighbor has four dogs that never stop barking.

5. We live next to the busiest traffic street in the whole area, and trucks roar past at all hours.

Did you choose numbers one, four, and five because these have specifics about noise? For number two, 30 houses might be noisy, but not necessarily—the houses might be empty or have no children or pets living there. Number three doesn't say what time of day the garbage collectors come or how they create noise.

Standards and Benchmarks: 1A, 1B, 1C, 1D, 2A, 2B, 2C, 3A, 3I, 3J, 3K

Developing Good Support

For each of the following sentences, circle the controlling idea and write three examples of support.

1. **Helena is a good friend since I can always depend on her.**

   A. _____

   _____

   B. _____

   _____

   C. _____

   _____

2. **Exercise is a productive way to lose weight.**

   A. _____

   _____

   B. _____

   _____

   C. _____

   _____

3. **The mall is a great place to spend the day with your friends.**

   A. _____

   _____

   B. _____

   _____

   C. _____

   _____

4. **Teenage boys like horror movies because they enjoy being scared.**

   A. _____

   _____

   B. _____

   _____

   C. _____

   _____

Effective Sentence Order

Ordering Sentences by Time

Some expository paragraphs are organized according to time. Usually this means writing examples or occurrences from the first instance that occurred to the last. Look at this example.

> Yesterday was the worst day I ever spent in middle school. From the beginning of that day when I arrived late at school, everything went wrong. My first period teacher chose me to answer the hardest math question I ever heard, and I had no idea of the answer. In second period, I sat in some gum stuck to the seat of my desk. At morning break I had a fight with my best friend. I managed to get through until lunch without anything terrible happening. But on the way to the table at lunch, I dropped my tray in front of the entire school. After school, I missed the bus and had to walk home alone. It was the kind of day I never want to have again.

Notice how the paragraph moves through the school day. Can you find the words that move the paragraph? They are called *transitions*. "From the beginning of the day" is the first one. Others are "first period" and "second period." Find at least two more and write them on the lines below.

Transitions

1. _____

2. _____

3. _____

Here are some other transition words we can use when writing in time order.

- **only a few years after**—Only a few years after I was born, my mom had another baby.

- **not long after this**—Not long after this I learned how to skateboard.

- **finally**—Finally, she was awarded the prize she had worked so hard to get.

- **then**—Then, we took a drive to the city center.

- **first, second, next, last**—These are all good transition words to use when writing sentences in order of time.

Standards and Benchmarks: 1D, 2D

Effective Sentence Order *(cont.)*

Ordering Sentences by Time *(cont.)*

Notice how the transition words are used in this example:

> Going to the movies is a great way for me to spend my free time. First, I enjoy getting out of the house. Second, I appreciate seeing a film on a huge screen so I don't miss any of the action. Third, snacks at a movie seem to taste better than anywhere else. Next, it is fun to hear the reaction of the audience to the comedy or horror on the screen. Last, I don't have to listen to anyone in my family trying to talk to me while I am trying to concentrate. There are many things I like about going to the movies.

On the lines below, write the transitional words in the paragraph about movies.

1. _____
2. _____
3. _____
4. _____
5. _____

Now write a series of sentences in a paragraph of your own, linking them together with transition words or phrases. Try to use transitional expressions different from the ones used in the paragraph above. After you have finished, underline your transitional words or phrases.

_____
_____
_____
_____
_____
_____
_____

Standards and Benchmarks: 2B, 2C, 3A

Effective Sentence Order *(cont.)*

Putting Sentences in Order

Read the following topic sentence and supporting details. Rearrange the support so it is in its most logical position and write the complete paragraph below.

Topic Sentence: During the 1960s, some of the most famous Broadway musicals became movies that won the Academy Award for best picture.

1. In 1961, *West Side Story,* a musical about rival gangs in New York, not only won best picture but two acting awards as well.

2. This trend ended in 1970 when the British musical *Oliver* took home the big award.

3. Only a year later, in 1965, the best picture award was won by *The Sound of Music,* one of the most popular and biggest money-making pictures of all time.

4. Only a few years later, in 1964, *My Fair Lady,* which many consider the very best musical of all time, won the Oscar.

_____

_____

_____

_____

_____

_____

_____

_____

_____

_____

_____

_____

Challenge: Write a concluding sentence for the paragraph.

Standards and Benchmarks: 1D, 2C, 2D, 3F, 3I

Effective Sentence Order *(cont.)*

Adverbial Phrases of Time and Sequence

There are many phrases that will help you as you write expository paragraphs and essays. Some are used when we are ordering writing by time or sequence.

Following are a few of the most common:

- **after** + time—**After 11:00 A.M.**, it is too late to leave for work.
- **before** + time—**Before 6:00 P.M.**, no one will be at the concert.
- **by** + time—Meet me in front of the museum **by 3:00 P.M.**
- **at** + time—**At noon**, all the restaurants are full.
- **after** + noun—**After the movies**, I want to go home.
- **before** + noun—**Before the beginning** of the game, the fans were quiet.
- **during** + noun—The crowd was on their feet **during the final seconds**.

The second main group uses words we looked at on the pages 74 and 75:

- **first, second, next, then, last, finally**

Fill in the blanks in the following paragraph with the appropriate adverbial expression of time or sequence from the list above.

Every fan in town was excited about the annual high school championship football game. _____ one o'clock everyone was in their seats. _____ the band played "The Star-Spangled Banner" and everyone stood and cheered. _____ our team came out. You could not hear yourself think with all the noise. _____ the game even started, my throat was hurting from screaming. _____ exactly three o'clock the referee held the football. _____ a little girl wandered out on the field, and everyone got very quiet. _____ about thirty seconds, a policeman came and took the girl into the stands. _____, the game began.

Now look at more transitional words that can be used to show sequence:

- **while**
- **when**
- **meanwhile**
- **at the same time**
- **simultaneously**

On the lines below, compose three or four sentences linked together with any combination of these transitions.

_____

_____

_____

_____

Standards and Benchmarks: 1D, 2D, 3A, 3I, 3J, 3K

Effective Sentence Order *(cont.)*

Expressions of Time and Sequence

Reread the essay "Restaurants Define San Francisco" on page 68. Locate the paragraph that uses time order for its sentences. Copy that paragraph below and circle the words or expressions (transitions) that help the reader to understand the order of events. On the lines below, explain how the circled words govern the sequence of ideas in the paragraph you selected.

Time Ordered Paragraph—"Restaurants Define San Francisco"

_____

_____

_____

_____

_____

_____

_____

_____

_____

_____

_____

_____

_____

_____

_____

_____

_____

_____

Standards and Benchmarks: 2D, 3G

Effective Sentence Order *(cont.)*

Prepositions in Time Expressions

❏ **At:** This word is used for time of day.
- The doctor needs to operate **at 7:00 AM**.
- First period begins **at 8:30 A.M.**
- Our family eats dinner **at 5:30 P.M.**

❏ **On:** This word is used for a particular day.
- My parents were married **on June 5th**.
- The school dance will be **on Saturday**.

❏ **In:** This word is used for a part of the day, month, season, or year.
- My brother begins work **in the afternoon**.
- **In January** there are many New Year's parades.
- Does it snow **in winter** where you live?
- My grandfather was born **in 1930**.

❏ **By:** This word indicates a period of time up to a certain point but not after.
- Most people eat dinner **by 7:00 P.M.**
- I expect everyone to arrive at the party **by noon**.

❏ **During:** This word is used for a certain span of time.
- **During the afternoon** I like to take a nap.
- Several people arrived **during the first act** of the play and disturbed us.

❏ **Until:** This word is used when an action is continued to a particular time.
- No one left the event-filled reunion picnic **until sundown**.
- The game was so exciting that all the fans stayed **until the end**.

❏ **Before:** This word is used to indicate a place or time in front of another object or event.
- He placed a candle **before the painting**.
- **Before sundown**, he lit every candle in the house.

Use the prepositions above to fill in the time expressions in the following paragraph.

_____ 7:30 P.M. everyone had voted in our town, although the polls were open _____ 8:00 P.M. _____ election day all the registered voters cast their ballots. Since we live on the eastern side of the country, TV reporters like to broadcast the outcome the same day. And even _____ the time that results are read, reporters try to predict the outcome of the entire national election. This happens _____ November of every election year.

Effective Sentence Order *(cont.)*

Ordering Sentences from Familiar to Unusual

Another way to develop paragraphs is by using examples that move from the familiar to less well-known examples. In this type of paragraph, the writer starts with examples that she feels everyone would know and ends with examples that the reader may not have thought about.

> It is important that parents read to their children from one to four years old. By listening, children develop an interest in stories. It prepares them for learning to read in first grade. It also provides a special time when a parent and child can develop closeness and sharing time. It makes children think in a different way than they do when they are watching TV or talking to their friends. All parents need to read to their kids.

Let's analyze this paragraph.

1. The writer begins with a topic sentence that has a controlling idea.

   Topic: parents reading to children

   Controlling Idea: important to read to children from ages one to four

2. The writer begins with a familiar example that almost everyone would consider:

   ". . . children (will) develop an interest in stories."

3. The writer continues with another familiar example that moves from the child's current age to a later one:

   ". . . prepares them for learning to read in first grade."

4. The writer starts to bring up less familiar ideas that many people might not think of:

   ". . . develop(ing) closeness and sharing time."

5. The writer's final example is the most unusual and perhaps the most controversial:

   ". . . makes children think in a different way. . . ."

6. The concluding sentence restates the topic in different words:

   "All parents need to read to their kids."

Standards and Benchmarks: 1A, 1D, 2C, 2D, 3A, 3I, 3J, 3K

Effective Sentence Order *(cont.)*

Ordering Sentences from Familiar to Unusual *(cont.)*

Which of the paragraphs in the essay "Restaurants Define San Francisco" on page 68 uses the familiar-to-unusual order for its sentences? Copy it below and then underline the specific examples you will use to explain your choice on the lines below.

Familiar-to-Unusual Paragraph—Restaurants Define San Francisco

_____

_____

_____

_____

_____

_____

_____

_____

_____

_____

_____

_____

_____

_____

_____

_____

Standards and Benchmarks: 1A, 1B, 1C, 1D, 1E, 1F, 2A, 2B, 2C, 2D, 3A, 3I, 3J, 3K

Effective Sentence Order *(cont.)*

Writing a Familiar-to-Unusual Paragraph

Choose one of the following topic sentences and practice writing a familiar-to-unusual paragraph, using the model on page 80 to help you organize.

1. **Children in elementary school should be encouraged to be on a sports team.**
2. **People enjoy living in small towns.**
3. **Learning to use the computer will help all students.**
4. **Boys should learn to cook just as much as girls.**

(Topic Sentence—with a Controlling Idea)

_____

_____

(Familiar Support)

_____

_____

(Familiar Support)

_____

_____

(Less Familiar Support)

_____

_____

(Unusual Support)

_____

_____

(Concluding Sentence—Which Restates the Topic)

_____

_____

Effective Sentence Order *(cont.)*

Saving the Best for Last

One last way an examples paragraph can be developed is to save the best or most important detail for last. Readers usually remember the last example they read more than the others, so one way to order the support is to place the most surprising or startling example at the end.

Study the following paragraph.

> Each state in the United States takes its name from a time when it was only a territory, and many of the most unusual names having to do with the geography of the region come from languages other than English. The huge state of Arizona takes its name from a Pima Indian word meaning "little spring place." Little Connecticut takes its name from a Mohican word that means "long river place." Vermont gets its name from two French words: vert (green) and mont (mountain). Perhaps the most surprising is Nevada, which is almost all desert, yet its name is Spanish for "snow-clad." Different languages have used the geographic landmarks of an area to create surprising state names.

Let's analyze this paragraph.

1. The writer begins with a topic sentence which has a controlling idea.

   - **Topic:** Each U.S. state was named when it was a territory.

   - **Controlling Idea:** Unusual names come from languages other than English and have to do with geography.

2. The writer first states an example that has to do with the geography: ". . . huge . . . Arizona takes its name from a Pima Indian word meaning 'little spring place.'"

   Though it is unusual, the writer feels it is not as strange as later examples.

3. The next example continues the idea of a surprising meaning: "Little Connecticut . . . from a Mohican word . . . 'long river place.'"

4. Moving to a different example, the writer shows that "Vermont gets its name from two French words. . . ." He points out that this state has a made-up name which uses geographical landmarks a bit more than previous ones.

5. Finally, the reader learns that Nevada's name means the opposite of what most think of when they consider the state:

   ". . . almost all desert, yet its name is Spanish for 'snow-clad.'"

6. The concluding sentence restates the topic sentence in different words:

   "Different languages have used the geographic landmarks of an area to create surprising state names."

Standards and Benchmarks: 2A, 2B, 2C, 2D

Effective Sentence Order *(cont.)*

Saving the Best for Last *(cont.)*

Which of the paragraphs in the essay "Restaurants Define San Francisco" on page 68 uses the saving-the-best-for-last order? Copy that paragraph and underline the appropriate examples. On the lines below, explain how these examples support your choice.

Saving-the-Best-for-Last Paragraph—Restaurants Define San Francisco

_____

_____

_____

_____

_____

_____

_____

_____

_____

_____

_____

_____

_____

_____

Standards and Benchmarks: 1A, 2B, 2C, 2D, 3A, 3J, 3K

Effective Sentence Order *(cont.)*

The Order-of-Importance Paragraph

Put the following sentences in the most appropriate sequence for an order-of-importance paragraph. Add your own topic sentence and concluding sentence. You can change any of the sentences you wish in order to make the writing sound more like you.

Supporting Sentences

1. Making your own Christmas presents can show others how much you care.
2. The maker has a feeling of accomplishment.
3. You can save money and get a one-of-kind present not found anywhere else.
4. Making your own presents allows you, the creator, to gain experience making an article with your own hands.

(Topic Sentence with a Controlling Idea)

_____

_____

(Support)

_____

_____

(Support)

_____

_____

(Surprising Support)

_____

_____

(Most Surprising Support)

_____

_____

(Concluding Sentence which Restates the Topic)

_____

_____

Effective Sentence Order *(cont.)*

Transitions

We have seen that there is more than one way to place sentences in an effective order. Effective order lets a writer express thoughts clearly and helps a reader to understand. Key words, called *transitions*, are the signals a good writer uses to show the order of how things happened. Transitional words help the reader move from idea to idea by stating or implying the connection between ideas. Transitions keep an essay on track and keep the reader focused on the order of events or thoughts. Following is a table of frequently used transitional words and phrases you may wish to use.

Transitions Table

Words That Show Sequence and Time		
after	next	before
during	earlier	later
at the same time	while	last
first, second, third, etc.	meanwhile	simultaneously

Words That Link Thoughts		
again	also	and
so	besides	further
furthermore	in addition	last
likewise	moreover	next

Words That Compare Ideas		
also	as well as	in the same way
likewise	similarly	resembling

Words That Contrast Ideas		
after all	although	even though
however	nevertheless	on the contrary
on the other hand	yet	

Words That Show Cause and Effect		
accordingly	due to	therefore
consequently	then	as a result
since	thus	because

Words That Emphasize		
definitely	certainly	indeed
in fact	surely	to be sure
truly	undoubtedly	without a doubt

Words That Summarize		
consequently	to sum up	in conclusion
in closing	finally	ultimately

The Examples Essay

Now that we have practiced the expository paragraph developed with examples, it is time to move on to the examples essay. You can use the same skills. However, instead of *one* paragraph, we will now write *five*. Instead of a topic sentence at the beginning of the paragraph, we will put it at the end of the first paragraph and call it the *"thesis statement."* We will have *three subtopic paragraphs* to develop with examples. Finally, we will conclude with *a summing-up paragraph* containing some main points to remember. In other words, the examples essay is basically organized exactly like an examples paragraph, for the paragraphs in the examples essay conform to the positions of the sentences in the examples paragraph.

Notice the following diagram:

Paragraph One
(*Thesis Statement*)

Paragraph Two
(*First Subtopic*)

Paragraph Three
(*Second Subtopic*)

Paragraph Four
(*Third Subtopic*)

Paragraph Five
(*Summing Up*)

The Examples Essay (cont.)

Let's study the following essay developed with examples.

The Importance of Keeping Up with the News

Some historians say the word "news" comes from the idea that it is information composed of what is "new." People enjoy hearing or reading the news to find out what is happening in the world right now. You can find out about what the personalities in your areas of interest are doing now. You can also find out information about local events. People who want to know the latest occurrences pay attention to the news.

The news allows a person to know the latest developments in the world. In almost every country there are English-speaking reporters ready to transmit important events. In minutes any incident can be shown on television, and every detail can be made available in the newspapers within a few hours. Whether it is a disaster in Asia or a scientific breakthrough in Europe, people who follow the news will know about it.

No matter what your interest, the news will give you information about the people involved. Every broadcast or newspaper has a section, for example, devoted to sports and entertainment. Newspaper readers can also find out the latest about newsmakers in science, politics, and business. Television news has segments devoted to showing pictures of people involved in all occupations. There is no doubt that a person who is interested in the news will know about the people who are making changes or creating the newest sensation.

Even those not interested in world events or global personalities will read the news for information affecting their city or community. Local newspapers and television news programs use much of their resources to report what is happening around their area. People can find out what is being done to make their city a safer and better place to live. They can see what exciting attractions and events are currently happening. The readers and viewers who only want to know the local news can have all their questions answered.

Almost all people have some interest in what is "new" in their world. It might be local occurrences, what is happening with their favorite personalities, or global developments. Whatever the readers' or viewers' interests, they can look to the news for the latest information.

The Examples Essay *(cont.)*

Let's analyze the essay "The Importance of Keeping Up with the News" by making an outline.

The Importance of Keeping Up with the News

I. (***Thesis Statement***) People who want to know the latest occurrences must pay attention to the news.

II. (***Subtopic***) Information about the latest in world developments

   A. Reporters all over the world transmit important events.

   B. Incidents can be shown on TV and details reported in newspapers quickly.

   C. Whether a disaster in Asia or a scientific breakthrough in Europe, it becomes known.

III. (***Subtopic***) Information about people, no matter what the interest

   A. Sections are devoted to sports and entertainment.

   B. Sections are devoted to the latest in science, politics, business.

   C. Pictures are available showing the people involved.

   D. Those people who are interested can know all about the newsmakers.

IV. (***Subtopic***) Information affecting the city or community

   A. TV and newspapers use resources to report on local happenings.

   B. Interested people can learn what is being done to make an area a safer and better place.

   C. Interested people can learn of exciting local happenings.

   D. Interested people can get local questions answered.

V. (***Conclusion***) News provides latest information, no matter what a reader's interest.

Standards and Benchmarks: 1A, 1B, 2B, 2C, 3A, 3F, 3G, 3I, 3J, 3K

The Examples Essay *(cont.)*

Your Own Thesis About the News

The writer of "The Importance of Keeping Up with the News" has used facts to prove her thesis about news. It is not the only thesis, however, that a person could use to write about the news. On the lines below, write a different thesis statement about a major problem with watching or reading about the news. Follow that with at least three subtopics you could use to support your thesis. Your teacher might want to brainstorm with the class about developing some of the possible theses.

(Thesis)

I. _____

_____

_____

(Subtopic 1)

II. _____

_____

_____

(Subtopic 2)

III. _____

_____

_____

(Subtopic 3)

IV. _____

_____

_____

(Conclusion)

V. _____

_____

_____

The Examples Essay *(cont.)*

Read the following student essay. Be prepared to outline it and answer questions concerning its development.

Finding a Wallet

Wallets are lost every day, and the person who finds one has to make a decision on what to do with it. There are many choices the finder has about how to handle this situation. Some people will keep the contents without questioning other possibilities. Others will take the money and return the credit cards and important papers to the owner. Still others might take the wallet to the police so that it can be returned untouched to the owner. Whatever action the finder takes with a wallet shows his personality and character.

The majority of people who find wallets will keep the wallet without question, which shows that these people think only of themselves. A person with this type of personality is very greedy and doesn't care who lost the wallet. He will immediately take the wallet home and throw into the trashcan everything that is of no interest to him. This type of finder will keep the money and anything else of value. He might even think about how to use the lost credit cards. The last thing on his mind would be to return the lost wallet to its owner. This person does not consider that taking the contents of this wallet is actually stealing.

Another type of person who is also greedy but considers the importance of the wallet to the owner will keep only the money and return the rest of the contents. He would look for the owner's address in the wallet and return it by mail without indicating his identity, so the owner would not be able to find him and accuse him of stealing the money. This finder might think he deserves a reward for returning the wallet and helps himself to the money. He might think that if he lost a wallet this is what the finder would do, so there is nothing wrong with him taking the money. He is more considerate than a person who throws away the wallet. He realizes that the credit cards, pictures, and rest of the wallet have importance to the owner. His taking of the money, however, is still not honest.

There is the honest person who, when finding the wallet, will immediately return it by mail or by turning it into the police. This person might think he will get a reward but is most concerned with doing what he thinks is the right thing to do. This is what he would like to happen if someone found his wallet. He would not feel right about taking something that did not belong to him. This person also gets a good feeling inside by returning the wallet to the owner without touching the contents. He has learned that it is better to be honest than dishonest, and his actions reflect this understanding.

When a person finds a wallet, he has many options. Whatever action he takes shows what sort of a person he is. His character is shown by what **he does** with the wallet. Whoever loses a wallet hopes that the person who finds it will be an honest one.

Standards and Benchmarks: 1B, 1D, 1F, 4G

The Examples Essay *(cont.)*

Outline the essay on page 91, "Finding a Wallet." Use the outline on page 89, "The Importance of Keeping Up with the News" as a model. Fill in the lines below or complete on your own paper.

Finding a Wallet

I. Thesis Statement

_____

II. Subtopic #1

_____

   A. support _____

   B. support _____

   C. support _____

III. Subtopic #2

_____

   A. support _____

   B. support _____

   C. support _____

IV. Subtopic #3

_____

   A. support _____

   B. support _____

   C. support _____

V. Conclusion

_____

_____

_____

_____

Standards and Benchmarks: 1D, 2C, 3A, 3I, 3J, 3K

The Examples Essay *(cont.)*

Answer the following questions about the essay on page 91, "Finding a Wallet."

1. What is the topic? What is the controlling idea?

   _____

   _____

2. How does each of the supporting paragraphs develop the thesis statement?

   _____

   _____

3. Are there enough examples in the essay to prove what the writer wishes to make the reader understand? Tell why.

   _____

   _____

4. Is the conclusion logical, considering the thesis statement and the support?

   _____

   _____

Need more practice? Try doing this page with the essay "Restaurants Define San Francisco" on page 68.

1. What is the topic? What is the controlling idea?

   _____

   _____

2. How does each of the supporting paragraphs develop the thesis statement?

   _____

   _____

3. Are there enough examples in the essay to prove what the writer wishes to make the reader understand? Tell why.

   _____

   _____

4. Is the conclusion logical, considering the thesis statement and the support?

   _____

   _____

Standards and Benchmarks: 1A, 1B, 1C, 1E, 1F, 2A, 2B, 2C, 2D, 3A, 3I, 3J, 3K

The Examples Essay *(cont.)*

Read the following thesis paragraph about food in a school cafeteria. Then study the examples in the list. Decide which examples have nothing to do with the thesis. Decide how to organize the rest of the examples into developmental paragraphs. Write an essay using the thesis paragraph given to you. Write the developmental paragraphs and the conclusion. You can change or add to any sentences below to improve your essay.

Thesis Paragraph

Children need good food to develop into strong adults. Most school cafeterias provide food that is not as good as it could be. Some cafeteria food has made students sick. Often the food available is not nutritious. Also, the food sometimes tastes very strange. Food in school cafeterias needs improvement.

For the Developmental Paragraphs:

1. The food in the cafeteria can make people sick. Last week I threw up after eating a burrito from the school cafeteria.

2. Many students bring their own lunch or buy items from machines so they can have food that tastes good.

3. Vegetables need to be more plentiful since now the lunches have too much fat content.

4. The cafeteria needs to be painted, and the uncomfortable chairs must be replaced.

5. The food in the cafeteria often tastes weird. The last hamburger I had at school couldn't have been real meat since it didn't taste like anything I had ever eaten.

6. I like the food at McDonald's.

7. The cafeteria should provide us with more ripe fruits. The plums are too hard and the apples too mushy.

8. The pizza at school, for example, tastes like cardboard.

9. The ladies who work in the cafeteria are nice to the students.

10. I heard my English teacher say that the last time he ate in the cafeteria, he got food poisoning.

11. We young people need to develop our bodies with better quality food, which the cafeteria doesn't provide.

12. My sister comes home almost every day with a stomachache.

13. Last month they served Jell-O® that had a flavor which couldn't have been made for humans to eat.

Standards and Benchmarks: 1D, 2C, 3A, 3I, 3J, 3K

The Examples Essay *(cont.)*

One student decided that sentences 4, 6, and 9 should not be included in the essay since these would not support the thesis paragraph. The student noted that her topic was *food in the school cafeteria* and the controlling idea was *needs improvement*. This is her essay.

Fix the Food

Children need good food to develop into strong adults. Most school cafeterias provide food that is not as good as it could be. Some cafeteria food has made students sick. Often the food available is not nutritious. Also, the food sometimes tastes very strange. Food in school cafeterias needs improvement.

To begin with, the food in the cafeteria can make people sick. Last week I threw up after eating a burrito from the school cafeteria. My sister comes home almost every day with a stomachache. I heard my English teacher say that the last time he ate in the cafeteria, he got food poisoning. The food must be changed so no one gets ill.

Furthermore, we young people need to develop our bodies with better quality food, which the cafeteria doesn't provide. The school cafeteria should provide us with more ripe fruits. The plums are too hard and the apples too mushy. Vegetables need to be more plentiful since now the lunches have too much fat content. Last week, I asked why there were no vegetables, and the cafeteria manager explained, "That's what the ketchup is!" Something has to be done about making the lunches more nutritious.

Finally, the food in the cafeteria often tastes weird. The last hamburger I ate at school couldn't have been real meat since it didn't taste like anything I had ever eaten. The pizza at school tastes like cardboard. Last month they served Jell-O that had a flavor which couldn't have been made for humans to eat. Many students bring their own lunch or buy items from machines so they can have food that tastes like it is supposed to.

Our school cafeteria needs improvement. Food shouldn't make people sick. It should be more healthful for us. It should not taste different than it looks. It is time for the adults at school to provide food the students will both enjoy and feel good about eating.

On the back of this page, compare your essay to this one. How are they similar? How are they different?

Standards and Benchmarks: 1A, 1B, 1C, 1E, 1F, 2A, 2B, 2C, 2D, 3A, 3A, 3I, 3J, 3K

The Examples Essay *(cont.)*

Now it is time for you to write your own examples essay. You have had a great deal of practice. Before you begin drafting your essay, use one of the brainstorming techniques we worked with on pages 36–44. Develop a controlling idea and appropriate examples for support. Making an outline first will make the writing of your essay much easier. You may begin your examples outline and essay on the back of this page or on another paper, as your teacher directs.

Following are some possible ideas that might work as topics for your first examples essay.

1. Develop an essay from your topic about the news.

2. Using the San Francisco essay on page 68, develop an essay about your city or state.

3. Have you ever lived somewhere else? Develop an essay about how you had to adjust to your new surroundings.

4. Develop an essay about your first day in middle school or a particular grade.

5. Develop an essay using one of the topics on page 82 (familiar-to-unusual order).

6. Clothes can tell a great deal about a person. Develop an essay about judging people from the clothes they wear.

7. Develop an essay telling why skateboarding (or any other sport) is or is not a good sport.

8. Develop an essay explaining the bad effects of the violence apparent in TV and film.

9. Develop an essay about the effects of humor used in commercials on TV.

10. Develop an essay about some other topic of your choice.

After selecting a topic for your essay, you may wish to use the graphic organizer on the following page to help plan the organization of your writing. (Alert readers may recognize this technique as one similar to the bubble graph technique shown earlier on page 41.)

Expository Essay Graphic Organizer

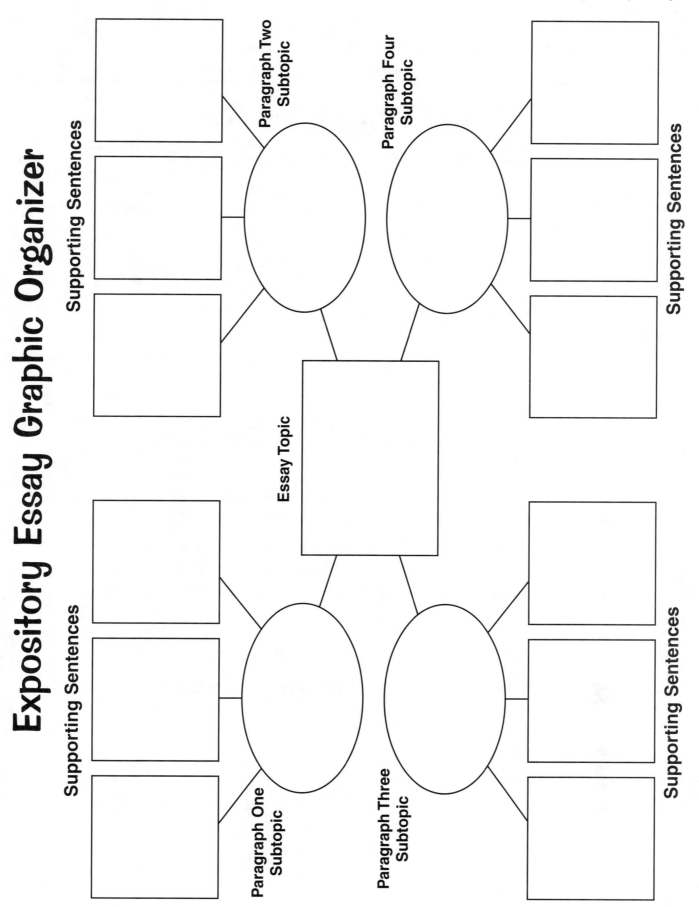

Supporting Sentences

Paragraph Two Subtopic

Paragraph Four Subtopic

Supporting Sentences

Essay Topic

Supporting Sentences

Paragraph One Subtopic

Paragraph Three Subtopic

Supporting Sentences

Standards and Benchmarks: 1D, 2C, 3A, 3I, 3J, 3K

Peer Checklist for Your Examples Essay

When you have finished your essay and have reread it to correct any obvious mistakes, give it to a classmate to read. The classmate is to read the essay carefully at least twice before answering the following questions.

Writer: _____

Reader: _____

Date: _____

1. What are the topic and controlling idea of the essay?

   _____

   _____

2. Do you have any suggestions about the introduction and/or thesis statement?

   _____

   _____

3. Does the first developmental (body) paragraph support the thesis? Any suggestions?

   _____

   _____

4. Do the second and third developmental paragraphs support the thesis? Any suggestions?

   _____

   _____

5. Do you have any suggestions about the conclusion?

   _____

   _____

6. What is the best part of this essay?

   _____

   _____

7. Which part of the essay needs the most improvement? Explain why.

   _____

   _____

The Comparison-and-Contrast Essay

Another very common type of expository essay is the comparison-and-contrast essay. Suppose you want to discuss how your brothers are alike or different. You would give specific information about each one and then discuss the similarities and differences. How would you write about your favorite teacher? One way would be to compare one teacher's characteristics with those of another to show how they are different. We use comparison and contrast every day. When we choose one restaurant over another or pick up a new pen, we have to consider our choices.

Read the following student essay to see how the writer uses comparison and contrast. This essay will be referred to throughout the following unit.

Remembering the Good Old Days

Three years ago I went back to visit my old home in Vietnam. That is where I grew up, a place I remember with love. It was where I played and spent time thinking about my future. However, the memories of my house and what I saw when I returned were not alike. I realize now that what I remember and what is real are not always the same.

When I arrived three years ago, I stood in front of my house and stared, trying to figure out why what I was seeing was not the same as the picture in my mind. The beautiful yellow house I remembered with strong walls was now crumbling and needed a paint job. The window of my bedroom was broken and had no curtains, but I don't remember any cracks in it when I lived there. And wasn't there a light blue covering? I played marbles and kicked a soccer ball under that window, but now there was only a muddy hole.

I tried to dig deeper into my memories of the place I lived in until I was ten years old. The tree now in front of my eyes could not have been the one I climbed every day to get away from my little brother and sister. I used to pretend to be Superman in that mighty tree. Sometimes I would take a book up there and read while cool breezes blew through the beautiful green leaves. Now I saw an ugly bundle of branches above a scarred trunk. It looked diseased.

I stared at the scene, wondering if my memory of the place could possibly have been this different from what I saw. My mom said the place looked just about the same as she remembered. I realize now that a ten-year-old looks at his world very differently from one who is 13. My home in Vietnam will never have the same pleasant memory it once had. I was sorry I had seen it again.

Standards and Benchmarks: 1D, 2C, 3A, 3I, 3J, 3K

The Comparison-and-Contrast Essay *(cont.)*

Answer the following questions about the "Remembering the Good Old Days" essay.

1. The writer is comparing what he remembers with what he sees. What is his topic? What is his controlling idea?

   _____

   _____

2. In the first developmental paragraph, what does the writer remember about his house? What does he see now? How are the two different?

   _____

   _____

   _____

   _____

3. In the second developmental paragraph, how does the writer compare his memory of the tree with the reality?

   _____

   _____

   _____

   _____

4. By comparing what he remembers and what he now sees, what does the writer realize about his memory?

   _____

   _____

   _____

   _____

5. Why does the writer say he wishes he hadn't visited his old house?

   _____

   _____

   _____

   _____

Standards and Benchmarks: 1A, 2C, 3A, 3I, 3J, 3K,

The Comparison-and-Contrast Essay *(cont.)*

What is the difference between *comparing* and *contrasting*?

The usual definitions are the ones given below.

Comparing: When you compare things in expository writing, you must use examples to show *how two things are alike and/or different*. You will want to point out the similarities and/or differences in several compelling ways.

Contrasting: When you contrast things in expository writing, you must use examples to show *how two things are different*. You will want to point out major ways the things are different.

Often this writing is simply called *comparison* since this term covers both similarities and differences. Be sure to consider whether it would be better to discuss how items are similar, how items are similar and different, or only how they are different (*contrast*).

Look at the list of pairs that follows at the bottom of this page. For each pair, decide whether it would be better to compare them or contrast them. Either answer is acceptable, but your explanation should clearly focus on the one you choose.

Example: The two baseball teams playing the last game of the World Series

Contrast—I think it is better to point out how the two teams are different since only one can win the championship.

1. The English class you had last year and the one you have this year

   _____

2. Your parents _____

3. You and your brother/sister/cousin/best friend _____

   _____

4. The two novels you last read _____

5. The two movies you last saw _____

6. Your two favorite TV shows _____

7. Your two favorite sports teams (which play the same sport) _____

   _____

8. Choosing whether to be a firefighter or a police officer _____

   _____

9. Your two favorite teachers _____

10. Your elementary school and your middle school _____

    _____

Standards and Benchmarks: 1A, 2B, 2C, 2D, 3A, 3I, 3J, 3K

The Comparison-and-Contrast Essay *(cont.)*

Before we start writing a comparison-and-contrast essay, let's begin by practicing the paragraph. A comparison-and-contrast paragraph will state its topic and controlling idea in the first sentence. Then in the middle sentence there will be examples to support the topic. The last sentence will conclude the short discussion. We will start our study with the comparison-and-contrast paragraph and, when we are comfortable, move on to writing an essay.

> It takes better physical conditioning to be a soccer player than a football player. First, a football player runs but is constantly stopping at the end of each play, whereas a soccer player runs practically the entire time he is playing. Secondly, football players must carry a great deal of weight on their bodies since they are required to knock down their opponents. Soccer players must remain thin and agile in order to move the ball down the field quickly. Finally, a soccer player must be in peak condition since he plays several games a week, whereas a football player usually plays only once a week. It is clear a soccer player requires better conditioning.

Questions

Answer these questions on the back of this page or on your own paper.

1. Is this mainly a comparison or a contrast paragraph? Explain.
2. What is the topic? The controlling idea?
3. What are the three supporting ideas for the topic?
4. How does the writer conclude the paragraph?
5. What is the writer comparing?
6. Can you think of another reason which would prove the argument?
7. Suppose you were asked to write another comparison paragraph about football and soccer. Can you think of another way to compare them? If so, how?

Sample Plan for a Comparison-and-Contrast Paragraph

Topic Sentence: The lessons learned in a public school are sometimes different from those a person might learn in a private school.

Comparisons

1. Learning to deal with many different ethnicities
2. Finding out about people who are in different economic positions
3. Having a more realistic view of the country

Standards and Benchmarks: 1A, 2C, 2D, 3A, 3I, 3J, 3K

The Comparison-and-Contrast Essay *(cont.)*

Look at the following topic sentences. See if you can write three comparisons/contrasts to help prove the topic.

Topic Sentence: It is more difficult to live in today's society than it was when my parents were young.

Comparisons:

1. _____

   _____

2. _____

   _____

3. _____

   _____

Topic Sentence: There are many more activities to do in the city than in the country.

Comparisons:

1. _____

   _____

2. _____

   _____

3. _____

   _____

Topic Sentence: When you are feeling sad, it is sometimes better to be with friends than with your parents.

Comparisons:

1. _____

   _____

2. _____

   _____

3. _____

   _____

Standards and Benchmarks: 1A, 2B, 2C, 2D, 3A, 3F, 3G, 3I, 3J, 3K

The Comparison-and-Contrast Essay *(cont.)*

Using the soccer/football paragraph on page 102 as a model, choose one of the outlines you have made and write a comparison/contrast paragraph in the space below. Exchange your paper with another student.

_____

_____

_____

_____

_____

_____

_____

_____

Directions to the reader: Answer the following questions about this paragraph.

1. What is the writer comparing?

_____

_____

2. Is the paragraph convincing? Explain why or why not.

_____

_____

3. Which is the strongest comparison? Why?

_____

_____

4. Write another comparison the writer could have used.

_____

_____

5. Do you feel this was a better comparison/contrast paragraph than the one you wrote? Why?

_____

_____

Standards and Benchmarks: 1A, 2C, 3A, 3I, 3J, 3K

The Comparison-and-Contrast Essay *(cont.)*

Comparing and contrasting is a process each of us performs every day. Every time you have a choice about what to have for breakfast, lunch, or dinner, you are comparing and contrasting. Think about the last time you were making a decision about what movie to see. You can see only one, so which do you choose? Following are some of the choices you may have been facing.

1. What time can I go, and what will be playing at that time?

2. Do I want to see the horror movie? the adventure movie? the comedy?

3. Which movie has the actors or actresses I most want to see?

4. Which movie has been out the longest? (After all, that one might be gone before I have a chance to see it if I don't go today.)

5. What have my friends said about the movies? Which friend's ideas of good movies are closest to mine?

6. Who should I ask to go with me? Will he or she want to see the same movie I do?

Now, of course, you may not actually ask yourself these questions out loud. In order to make a choice, however, your mind does go through the process of comparing and contrasting.

Suppose you go to a restaurant and are given a menu. What comparing and contrasting questions might you ask yourself? Write down five possible questions on the lines below.

1. _____

_____

_____

2. _____

_____

_____

3. _____

_____

_____

4. _____

_____

_____

5. _____

_____

_____

The Comparison-and-Contrast Essay *(cont.)*

Suppose you want to participate in both the drama club and the track team. However, you find out that you cannot be in both, for the drama club rehearses right after school and the track team practices at the same time. One way to make a decision is to create a chart like the one below, listing positive reasons to join each.

Drama Club	**Track Team**
1. I like to act.	1. I like to run.
2. The drama teacher has chosen a great play to perform.	2. The track coach has decided to travel to several meets.
3. All my friends are planning to audition.	3. I have the opportunity to meet some new friends.
4. The drama teacher is funny.	4. The track coach can teach me new skills.
5. This would definitely be enjoyable.	5. This would definitely be enjoyable.

What might your paragraph look like? Will it be a comparing paragraph or a contrasting one? Actually, it could be either, depending on how you decide to write it. Do you want to discuss how they are alike, different, or both?

Let's take a look at how each might be written.

Comparison Paragraph

Joining the drama club or the track team creates a dilemma when you can choose only one. They would both allow me to enjoy two of my favorite activities, acting and running. People say I have a talent for both. The teachers are both great people with much knowledge to share with their students. I love to perform, and each would give me the opportunity to show what I can do in front of an audience. Each has great activities planned for the upcoming year. This is a difficult choice.

Contrast Paragraph

It is difficult to make a decision on whether to participate in the drama club or the track team since they both meet at the same time. While the drama teacher has chosen a great play to present, the track coach has decided to travel to some super meets. All my friends have decided to audition for the play, but being on the track team will allow me to widen my circle of friends. Everyone knows how funny the drama teacher is, however the track coach knows so much and can teach me many new skills. I can join only one, so this is a difficult dilemma.

Standards and Benchmarks: 1A, 2B, 2C, 2D, 3A, 3F, 3G, 3I, 3J, 3K

The Comparison-and-Contrast Essay *(cont.)*

It is now time for you to try a comparison-and-contrast paragraph.

Choose one of the topics on page 101, make a chart, and write a comparing or contrasting paragraph. Perhaps you'll want to try both. Model your paragraph according to the ones on the previous page.

Before you start writing, fill in the following chart. (Look on page 106 for an example.)

Topic sentence with controlling idea: _____

_____

Subject #1 _____   *Subject #2* _____

After completing your chart above, write your paragraph(s) in the space below.

Standards and Benchmarks: 1A

The Comparison-and-Contrast Essay *(cont.)*

Look back to the comparison/contrast essay on "Remembering the Good Old Days" on page 99. Notice that the essay is not just about the differences between what the writer remembers and what he now sees. The controlling idea is more complicated. The thesis statement is *I realize now that what I remembered and what is real are not always the same.* This is a strong controlling idea that works in an essay. An essay, being longer than a paragraph, needs a thesis statement (*topic and controlling idea*) that can extend over its entire length. Not only is the writer explaining the difference between what used to be and what now is, he has also realized something important about the nature of memory.

Suppose you are asked to write an essay about two members of your family. You decide to discuss your sisters since they are different in many ways. However, just saying they are different is a bit weak, for there is no controlling idea. Why not start with a Venn diagram to plot how your sisters are both different and the same?

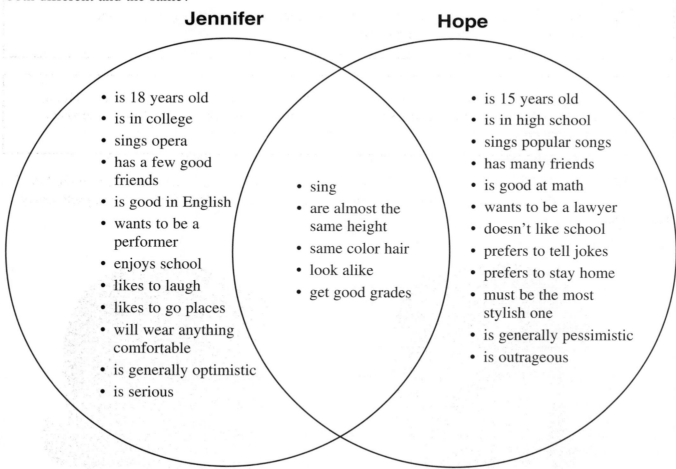

Jennifer

- is 18 years old
- is in college
- sings opera
- has a few good friends
- is good in English
- wants to be a performer
- enjoys school
- likes to laugh
- likes to go places
- will wear anything comfortable
- is generally optimistic
- is serious

- sing
- are almost the same height
- same color hair
- look alike
- get good grades

Hope

- is 15 years old
- is in high school
- sings popular songs
- has many friends
- is good at math
- wants to be a lawyer
- doesn't like school
- prefers to tell jokes
- prefers to stay home
- must be the most stylish one
- is generally pessimistic
- is outrageous

The Comparison-and-Contrast Essay *(cont.)*

Now that the list of characteristics is made, the writer needs to consider what the thesis statement will be. Notice that Jennifer is older but more serious. Hope is younger and cares more about what others think of her. However, they also have many characteristics in common. This will be a comparison-and-contrast essay since the two sisters are alike in some ways and different in others.

Let's try composing several possible thesis statements.

1. Jennifer and Hope are obviously sisters, but each has her own unique way of looking at life.

2. My sisters are sometimes mistaken for each other; however, anyone who knows them is surprised at their differences.

3. Although one of my sisters is serious and optimistic and the other is flighty and pessimistic, they have much in common.

4. One of my sisters, Jennifer, combines optimism with seriousness while the other, Hope, mixes pessimism with outrageousness—combinations which make my look-alike sisters a study in contrast.

Which of the possible thesis statements do you think works the best? Our writer decided on the last one since it seemed to contain the most information about the two subjects. Read the complete essay that appears on the page 110.

The Comparison-and-Contrast Essay *(cont.)*

You Can't Judge a Sister by Her Exterior

Sisters are never totally alike. Even if they resemble each other, they have their own characteristics. When others meet my sisters for the first time, there is always a comment about how similar they look. I know that they have more in common than their looks, but I see them as unique individuals. One combines optimism with seriousness while the other mixes pessimism with outrageousness—combinations which make my look-alike sisters a study in contrast.

Jennifer, the eighteen-year-old, has always been a serious-minded person yet is usually optimistic about life. She is a freshman in college and has known what her major would be since she was in middle school. She sings opera and wants to be a performer, so music is her field of study. When she calls home, her voice is full of excitement about all that she is doing. She says all her classes are great. She likes her roommate, who seems to share Jennifer's sense of style—that is, whatever is most comfortable. She even says, "The dorm food has been surprisingly good." She is having a super time, but her classes come first. Just as in high school, she studies first and then plays afterwards. All of her grades have been A's and B's so far. She has joined a small sorority, which is just like her. She likes a small group of good friends rather than having a large number of them. Jennifer is a person who takes her future in her own hands and makes the best of it, smiling all the while.

Hope, who has just turned 15, has often been mistaken for Jennifer's twin. She is about the same height with the same color hair and eyes. She, like her sister, thinks singing is the best activity. Hope's voice is much lower than her sister's, so she prefers popular music. She hasn't decided what she wants to do with her life except to make money. She dresses to make a statement, and if that means being uncomfortable, that's fine with her. Outrageous is the word for her clothes. She works hard in school but constantly complains loudly about all the pressure. She laughs a great deal but prefers to be the one telling the jokes, and they are usually shocking. The phone rings constantly, and it is always for her. She has more friends than anyone else in the family. She talks about going away to college, but now when she has the opportunity to go out, she often would rather stay at home. She can be very quiet and tends to look on the dark side of life. "Life isn't fair," is her favorite saying.

My sisters are look-alikes who are so very different. Jennifer is serious about her goals and is optimistic about making them happen. Hope is hilariously outrageous with her jokes and clothes but has an unhappy streak. Sometimes I wonder how two people who look so alike and have many of the same interests can be so different in personality. They are sort of like the MAC and PC. They look almost the same, but each has its own way of getting things done.

Standards and Benchmarks: 1D, 2C, 3A, 3I, 3J, 3K

The Comparison-and-Contrast Essay *(cont.)*

Answer these questions about the comparison/contrast essay about the sisters on page 110.

1. How does the title provide the reader with a clue to the subject of the essay?

   _____

   _____

2. The first sentence in an essay should not be wasted. What do you think about the first sentence of this essay? How does it show a sense of organization?

   _____

   _____

3. Although the thesis paragraph is well organized, which sentence could be left out without hurting the meaning? Why?

   _____

   _____

4. How is the paragraph developed—in block or step-by-step form? (Look ahead to pages 114 and 115 for help.) Explain how you know.

   _____

   _____

5. In what paragraph is a specific comparison made? Why do you think the writer has waited to start making the comparison until this paragraph?

   _____

   _____

6. Read between the lines and explain how the writer feels about each of the sisters? (What is the tone of this essay?)

   _____

   _____

7. What does the writer compare the sisters to in the conclusion? What is your opinion of this comparison? Can you think of a different comparison?

   _____

   _____

   _____

The Comparison-and-Contrast Essay *(cont.)*

Sometimes you are asked to compare characters or situations from two novels you have read for your class. Usually these novels have many things in common but are also different in important ways.

The following page contains an example of an essay comparing characters from Fred Lipson's *Old Yeller* and Jerry Spinelli's *Maniac Magee*. First, look at the Venn diagram:

Travis (Old Yeller)

Maniac (Maniac Magee)

Similarities

Travis (Old Yeller)
- Lived with parents
- Parents were loving
- Matured on ranch
- Had one younger brother
- Lived in Texas, 1870–1880
- Only met one new person
- Had to deal with difficult animals
- Favorite animal died

Similarities
- Forced to mature by life situation
- Lived in U.S.
- Cared about others
- Had many difficulties
- Had to deal with death
- Matured into a compassionate young man

Maniac (Maniac Magee)
- Lived with uncle/aunt
- Uncle/aunt were hateful
- Matured on his own
- Had no siblings
- Lived in Pennsylvania
- Met many new people
- Had to deal with bigots
- Favorite person died

The Comparison-and-Contrast Essay *(cont.)*

Growing Up Quickly

There are many novels that have the theme of children growing into young adults. Two of the most interesting, although the action occurs in two different centuries, are *Old Yeller* by Fred Gipson and *Maniac Magee* by Jerry Spinelli. In each, a boy must grow up quickly due to his life circumstances. Travis and Maniac, though different in their situations, are similar in that they are forced to grow up too quickly.

Travis in *Old Yeller* must take over the male leadership role for his family when his father must take cattle to market. Maniac voluntarily leaves his impossible living environment with his uncle and aunt. Travis lives in Texas following the Civil War while Maniac travels through Pennsylvania in the 1980s. In different times and different places, each of these young boys is forced to take on heavy responsibilities.

Travis and Maniac are forced to act like mature adults before they are ready to do so. Travis has to care for the animals on the ranch and must stop his chores when he is nearly killed by the pigs. Maniac must deal with racial problems and must leave the African-American family he loves because of the prejudice of others. If they had been older, Travis and Maniac might have had a better understanding of their difficult situations and not have become so tangled in such problems.

Both of the characters must deal with death of a being very close to them. Travis must kill his beloved dog, Yeller, when it becomes sick with rabies. Maniac must deal with the loss of Grayson, the person who helped him when he most needed to be cared for. Both boys had a great deal of trouble dealing with these deaths, but learned a great deal. At the close of their stories, they have become mature enough to understand and appreciate that what they once had will help them move on with their lives.

Travis and Maniac become compassionate young men through their trials. Travis learns what it means to be an adult and run a ranch. Maniac learns that people have more in common than they have in differences. In both novels, the main character becomes a caring person through the lessons he has learned.

The Comparison-and-Contrast Essay *(cont.)*

Comparison/contrast essays are often written in two major styles—subject-by-subject and feature-by-feature. (These are also called *block form* and *step-by-step form*.) Subject-by-subject form is the style described when all the features of one subject are discussed and then all the features of the other are discussed. The two subjects being compared are discussed separately. In the "Growing Up Quickly" essay, a subject-by-subject style would have us first write all about Travis, for example, and then write all about Maniac. In feature-by-feature style, however, both subjects are discussed together. One particular feature is chosen, and both subjects are then discussed, focusing on their connection to that feature.

The novel essay "Growing Up Quickly" is written in the feature-by-feature form. In the "You Can't Judge a Sister by Her Exterior" essay, the subject-by-subject form is used. Which type is used in the memory essay on page 99? If you said feature-by-feature, you are right. Continuously throughout the essay, the writer compares each feature that he remembers with what he sees now.

Look at the following outlines:

Subject-by-Subject Form

I. **Introduction**

II. **Subject A**
   A. feature 1
   B. feature 2
   C. feature 3

> Part II may be one paragraph discussing three different features or three paragraphs, each about a different feature of subject (or person) A.

III. **Subject B**
   A. feature 1
   B. feature 2
   C. feature 3

> Part III should follow the same pattern as Part II in the box, except it will discuss features of subject (or person) B.

IV. **Conclusion**

Feature-by-Feature Form

I. **Introduction**

II. **Feature 1**
   A. subject A
   B. subject B

> Part II will generally be one paragraph discussing the same feature for each subject (or person).

III. **Feature 2**
   A. subject A
   B. subject B

> Part III should follow the same pattern as Part II in the box above.

IV. **Feature 3**
   A. subject A
   B. subject B

> Part IV should follow the same pattern as Part III in the box above.

V. **Conclusion**

The Comparison-and-Contrast Essay *(cont.)*

Let's see how the last two essays would fit into the appropriate outline:

You Can't Judge a Sister . . .

I. Introduction (Thesis: . . . sisters a study in contrast)

II. Jennifer

    A. outlook

    B. interests

    C. dressing

    D. friends

> These are the "features" shown in the subject-by-subject form outline on page 114. Jennifer represents subject A in that outline.

III. Hope

    A. outlook

    B. interests

    C. dressing

    D. friends

> Hope is subject B in the outline on page 114. Notice that the features in this paragraph are in exactly the same order as in Part II above.

IV. Conclusion

Growing Up Quickly

I. Introduction (Thesis: . . . forced to grow up too quickly)

II. Male Leadership Role

    A. Travis

    B. Maniac

> Travis and Maniac are subject A and subject B of the feature-by-feature form on page 114.

III. Acting Like Mature Adults

    A. Travis

    B. Maniac

> Notice that for this feature, Travis and Maniac are discussed in the same order as in Part II above.

IV. Dealing with Death

    A. Travis

    B. Maniac

> For the feature "Dealing with Death," notice again that we discuss Travis first and Maniac second.

V. Conclusion

How do you decide which form to use? You must ask yourself whether you are comparing *subjects* or *features*. If it is mostly comparing the subjects, then the first form will serve your essay well. If you are mainly comparing features, then use the second form. Could each of these essays been written with the other form? Yes; however, subject-by-subject usually works better if you are mostly trying to show differences (*contrasting*). Feature-by-feature works best if you are mainly showing similarities (*comparing*). However, no matter which you choose, both will give your essay a clear organization. Can you see how the Venn diagram form helps you to organize a comparison/contrast essay?

Standards and Benchmarks: 1A, 3I, 3J, 3K

The Comparison-and-Contrast Essay *(cont.)*

Writing a Comparison/Contrast Essay

Now it is time for you to write a comparison/contrast essay. Use one of the topic choices on page 101, or use another of your own selection. Check with your teacher on your topic choice. Before you begin writing your essay, fill out the Venn diagram below.

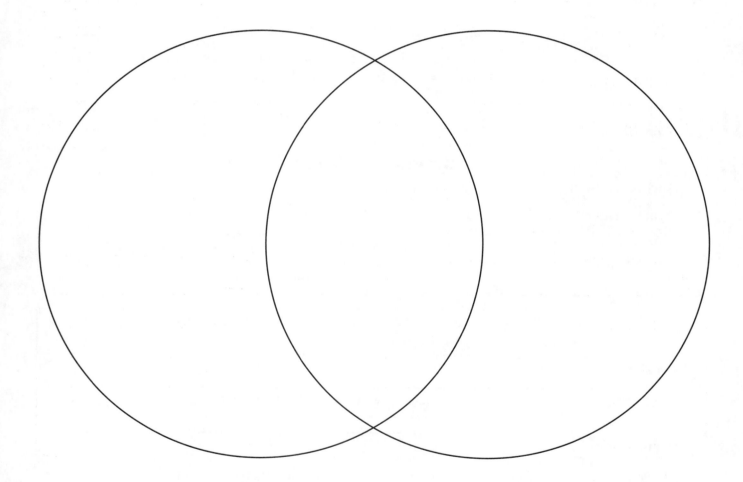

Standards and Benchmarks: 1A, 1F, 2B, 2C, 2D, 3A, 3F, 3G, 3I, 3J, 3K

The Comparison-and-Contrast Essay *(cont.)*

Writing a Comparison/Contrast Essay *(cont.)*

Now that you have your Venn diagram finished, you must decide whether you will use the *subject-by-subject* or *feature-by-feature* form. Try each of the outlines to see which is better for your topic. After finishing the two outlines, answer the following.

1. Following are two possibilities for my thesis statement:

    a. _____

    b. _____

2. The one I think would be the best is _____ because_____

    _____

    _____

3. The way I have decided to compare/contrast my two subjects is to use the _____ -by-
    _____ method. This would be best since _____

    _____

    _____

Now it is time to use your outline to compose your essay.

Compose your thesis paragraph (introduction) below and let your teacher comment on it before you continue.

_____
_____
_____
_____
_____

Teacher Comments:

_____

_____

_____

Standards and Benchmarks: 1D, 2B, 2C, 2D, 3A, 3I, 3J, 3K

Peer Checklist for Your Comparison-and-Contrast Essay

When you have finished your essay and have reread it to correct any obvious mistakes, give it to a classmate to read. The classmate is to read the essay carefully at least twice before answering the following.

Writer: _____

Reader: _____

Date: _____

1. What is the thesis statement of the essay?

   _____

   _____

2. What is the writer's attitude about the topic?

   _____

   _____

3. Has the writer chosen the subject-by-subject or feature-by-feature form?

   _____

   _____

4. Which do you think is the most effective developmental (body) paragraph? Explain why you chose this one.

   _____

   _____

5. Do you have any suggestions about the conclusion?

   _____

   _____

Return the paper to the writer.

Writer: Now that you have read the peer comments, what could you do to improve your essay?

_____

_____

The Argumentative Essay

Review

Whether one writes an example essay or a comparison/contrast essay, all good expository essays make use of certain basic principles:

1. **In the introduction part of an essay, there should be a thesis statement** of some kind, announcing the topic and a controlling idea or attitude toward the topic. This thesis statement will usually be found in the first paragraph of the essay, frequently appearing as the last sentence in that paragraph.

2. **There should then be at least two or three paragraphs that support the thesis statement** with strong specific examples to prove the writer's point or controlling idea.

3. **The sentences in each paragraph** (and even the paragraphs themselves) **should be connected by appropriate words or phrases of sequence**. These words and phrases that connect your ideas and make sequences clear to the reader are called *transitions*.

4. If the essay is comparison/contrast, you **may organize the paragraphs in subject-by-subject form or in feature-by-feature form.**

5. **The conclusion paragraph of the essay will often summarize the points** made in previous paragraphs and then restate, support, or prove the thesis statement that appeared at the beginning of the essay.

Up to this point, you have been writing essays that use examples to explain or analyze and essays that compare and contrast. Now we will look at a different type of expository writing.

Argumentative Writing

Argumentative writing tries to *convince* or *persuade*. This is the type of writing you would use to discuss a controversial subject. It might be used in a speech where the speaker is attempting to persuade the listener to change his or her mind.

When you use argumentative writing, you must be aware of your reader. Since you must convince the reader that your position is the correct one, it might be best to assume the reader does not agree with you. How will you persuade him or her? Superior argumentative writing will bring up points that a person opposed might feel are good arguments and then attempt to answer those arguments in a way that will change the reader's mind.

Read the student essay on page 120 and notice how the writer uses argumentation. This essay will be referred to throughout the following unit.

The Argumentative Essay *(cont.)*

Don't Get That Driver's License

Although most middle school students dream of the day they will get their driver's license, there are many nightmares they might not consider which come with that 'wonderful' document. The cost of running an automobile, added responsibilities, and the chance of getting into an accident are important considerations. When a prospective driver considers these negatives, the thought of driving becomes much less attractive.

Most people who want to drive think about the fun of having their own set of wheels without considering the cost of those wheels. Gas is continually becoming more and more expensive. One gallon might only cost $1.80, but filling up the tank will be over 20 dollars. A new driver will usually have an older car which will be in need of constant repair. A brake job alone could be over two-hundred dollars, and new tires could run another two hundred. If something big like a transmission or carburetor needs replacing, the cost could be so much that the driver might not have the money to pay for it.

Now your parents probably take you wherever you need to go. When you can drive yourself, you won't have to rely on them, but they might start relying on you to run errands they used to do. You might be the one who has to pick up your younger brother or sister from sports practice or music lessons. Your mom often needs an item from the supermarket, and it will be easier for her to send you than leave the house herself. Your dad might be involved in fixing a broken appliance and will need to send you to the hardware store to get the equipment he needs.

Another consideration is getting in an accident. Every time you get behind the wheel, there is a chance of having an accident. There is insurance to handle the cost of the accident, but it is not so easy to get over the emotional regret of possibly hurting someone. Many young people have had to deal with the injury or even death of a friend or relative, even when it was another driver's fault. Although most people don't think they will ever get in an accident, it unfortunately happens all the time. A car travels with tremendous force and can injure or kill even when the driver is very careful. A sixteen-year-old student is very young to deal with this possible situation.

Driving our friends along a beach or mountain road is a dream most of us have had at one time or another. However, there are responsibilities that come with that dream and with the driver's license needed for it. It is important to consider these responsibilities when thinking about learning to drive. Driving is a skill we all want, but many students are waiting until they are a bit more mature before they take this step.

Standards and Benchmarks: 1C, 1D, 3A, 3I, 3J, 3K

The Argumentative Essay *(cont.)*

Don't Get That Driver's License *(cont.)*

Answer these questions about this essay.

1. What is the thesis statement of this argumentative essay?

   _____

   _____

2. What does the writer think that most of the readers feel about learning how to drive?

   _____

   _____

   _____

3. What do you feel is the strongest argument the writer makes against getting a driver's license at a young age? Why is this the strongest argument?

   _____

   _____

   _____

   _____

4. What is the writer's weakest argument? Why is it weak?

   _____

   _____

   _____

5. Can you think of a way to strengthen this weak argument?

   _____

   _____

   _____

6. Do you think this essay would convince young people to reconsider getting a driver's license? Why?

   _____

   _____

   _____

The Argumentative Essay *(cont.)*

Let's consider some controversial subjects many of your classmates might be considering.

1. Smoking or Drug Use
2. Going Steady
3. Cutting Classes
4. Telling the Truth

These are subjects you probably have strong feelings about. Remember that your feelings are not necessarily the same as your classmates. Some might have very different ideas about these subjects. Suppose you are asked to write a paragraph about why it is detrimental to smoke tobacco. There are many health reasons for why it is not smart to smoke. You are aware that your classmates know these reasons, and yet some still choose to smoke. You want to persuade them that smoking is a mistake, and since you think that they already know about the long-term effects of smoking, you decide to concentrate on other reasons that might get through to them. First you brainstorm:

1. Smoking smells bad, and it makes your breath stink.
2. Many of your friends will not want to hang around you if you smoke.
3 Someone in authority might catch you, and you will be in trouble.
4. Smoking is a very expensive activity that will leave you no money for other activities you want to enjoy.

Here is a paragraph based on the brainstorming.

> Because of all the long-range effects that everyone knows about, smoking is not a positive activity; however, there are other problems that make a difference right now to a young student. First, smoking smells bad to those around you, and it makes your breath stink. Secondly, there are some of your friends who will not hang around with you if they know you smoke. Third, an adult could catch you smoking, and you could get suspended or expelled from school. Finally, the cost of smoking is high for young people who don't have much money for all the activities they enjoy. Smoking will certainly change your life—and not for the better.

Argumentative writing must have a strong attitude:

- What is the attitude of this writer?
- Who is his audience?
- What does the writer hope that the reader will consider after he reads the paragraph?
- Can you think of other reasons the writer could have included? any that could have been left out?

Standards and Benchmarks: 1A, 1E, 2C, 3A, 3I, 3J, 3K

The Argumentative Essay *(cont.)*

Now that you know what argumentative writing is, let's try to decide which of the following are appropriate subjects for an argumentative paragraph or essay.

Put an "X" next to the topic sentences which could be used in an argumentative paragraph.

_____ 1. The rainfall last year was the heaviest on record.

_____ 2. Students should have to be at least 18 before they can be issued a driver's license.

_____ 3. Our district needs at least one new high school and two new middle schools.

_____ 4. Students should be able to decide which teachers they want, especially in English, math, and science.

_____ 5. Most of the kids I've met in this school are friendly.

_____ 6. My two favorite types of food are Italian and Chinese.

_____ 7. Our middle school needs to have more clubs so students have more opportunities to express their individualism.

_____ 8. Michelle should work harder in school rather than be so concerned with her friends.

_____ 9. After Mom works hard at her job all day, she has to come home and make dinner, do laundry, and make sure I finish my homework.

_____ 10. Basketball is my favorite sport since the action never stops.

Choose two of the topic sentences that would *not* work well for argumentative writing and revise them so that they are argumentative.

First Choice:

_____

_____

_____

_____

Second Choice:

_____

_____

_____

_____

Standards and Benchmarks: 1A, 1E, 2C, 3A, 3I, 3J, 3K

The Argumentative Essay *(cont.)*

Some subjects are argumentative and others are not. The thesis "In the United States, hurricanes have caused the most severe damage to families living in Florida" is not argumentative. It is either true or not true, and a bit of research can prove it one way or the other. However, a thesis such as "Hurricanes are more devastating than earthquakes" *cannot* be proved with certainty either way, and it is, therefore, argumentative.

Look at the following thesis statements and decide whether they are argumentative or not. Place an "A" in the blank if the thesis is argumentative. Write a "No" in the blank if it is not argumentative.

_____ 1. Many people prefer cats to dogs as pets.

_____ 2. Cats make better pets than dogs.

_____ 3. Arizona has some of the most beautiful scenery in the western United States.

_____ 4. Arizona's national parks are more beautiful than those in Utah.

_____ 5. Our state university has the best sports program.

_____ 6. The school library needs a computer system with Internet access.

_____ 7. No student should have to take physical education unless he or she wants to.

_____ 8. Students learn best in a clean and comfortable environment.

_____ 9. My family enjoys Thanksgiving more than any other holiday.

_____ 10. The best place to have a family vacation is in a warm climate.

You will notice that some of the thesis statements are clearly argumentative and others are more difficult to figure out. Look at number six. Is it argumentative? Write down your reasons for making the decision you did.

Take a class vote on number six and discuss why students felt this one was argumentative or not.

_____

_____

_____

_____

_____

_____

_____

Standards and Benchmarks: 1A, 1D, 1J, 2B, 2C, 2D, 3A, 3I, 3J, 3K

The Argumentative Essay *(cont.)*

Using the paragraph on smoking (page 122) as an example, write your own argumentative paragraph. First, brainstorm some topics with your class.

Choose a Topic: _____

Brainstorm some possible reasons for your argument:

1. _____

2. _____

3. _____

4. _____

What might be your thesis statement? Write your paragraph below.

_____
_____
_____
_____
_____
_____

Now to prove that this is truly an argumentative paragraph, how might someone else argue the other side?

_____
_____
_____
_____
_____
_____

Trade your paragraphs with other students. On the back of the other student's page, comment on the paragraph. Is it argumentative? Which is the best argument? Which needs improvement?

The Argumentative Essay *(cont.)*

The American Declaration of Independence is one of the most famous argumentative essays in the world. It asserts that "a decent respect to the opinions of mankind" requires the writers to persuade mankind of the correctness of the colonists' resolve to separate from Britain and become self-governing states. In fact, the document has been so persuasive that independence movements in a number of countries other than the United States have used Thomas Jefferson's famous words as an inspiration to call for their own self-government.

Many historic speeches—what we might call "spoken essays"—are also argumentative. The speaker usually wants to persuade the listener of the "rightness" of his or her position.

Over the span of the last 200 years, some of these argumentative speeches have become woven into the fabric of the English language, and whole chunks of them have passed into our common culture. Brief quotes and references to any one of these appear almost daily in the media and in common conversation. These references are almost always used to summon up rich emotional and historic meanings that bind us together as a people. From Patrick Henry to Martin Luther King, Jr., the argumentative "spoken essay" has exerted great influence on our lives, lifting up our spirits and calling upon the best in the human heart. To better understand the argumentative process, you might want to read or listen to one or more of the following speeches.

❏ **Patrick Henry**—"Speech to the Virginia Convention" (1775). This is the famous "Give me liberty or give me death" speech. Henry tries to persuade the Virginia legislature to prepare for war against the British.

❏ **Sojourner Truth**—"Ain't I a Woman?" (1851). Truth speaks on Women's Rights.

❏ **Abraham Lincoln**—"Gettysburg Address" (1863). Lincoln explains to a war-weary republic why the Civil War must continue.

❏ **Frederick Douglass**—"Untie His Hands" (1865). In this speech Douglass explains why Blacks should be given equality.

❏ **Susan B. Anthony**—"On a Woman's Right to Vote" (1873). Anthony argues the reasons why a woman should have this right, the same as a man does.

❏ **Chief Joseph**—"I Will Fight No More Forever" (1877). Chief Joseph of the Nez Percé tribe explains why his people will surrender.

❏ **Winston Churchill**—"Blood, Sweat, and Tears" (1940). Churchill argues the reasons for Great Britain to continue fighting in World War II.

❏ **John Fitzgerald Kennedy**—"Inaugural Address" (1961). Kennedy explains the reasons the United States citizens must work together and serve the country.

❏ **Martin Luther King, Jr.**—"I Have a Dream" (1963). On August 28 in Washington, D.C., King eloquently appeals to the ultimate justice of the human heart and the deep desire for equality and compassion based not on the color of skin but on the content of character.

The Argumentative Essay *(cont.)*

Each of the speeches listed on the previous page is similar to an argumentative essay in that each argues its points and tries to persuade the listeners. The writer of a good speech or a good essay will consider the questions the opposing side would have so he or she can answer those who do not agree.

Imagine Abraham Lincoln considering a speech he must make to the relatives of thousands of men who have died fighting for the Union in the Civil War. In 1863, the war is not close to being resolved. The South has better generals and better trained fighting units. As president, Lincoln knew he had to instill in his listeners the will to continue this war that had divided the country. Many of the people he was talking to were not behind the Union as strongly as they had been when the war had begun over two years before.

As Lincoln planned the speech, he might have made the following chart.

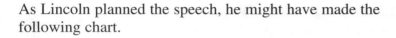

Pro

1. The Union is right to abolish slavery.

2. The United States must be preserved.

3. Liberty is more important than anything else.

4. If we stop the war now, the men who have died will have died for no reason.

Con

1. Many Northerners don't believe abolishing slavery is a strong enough reason to lose their sons and husbands.

2. It is better to make peace with the South and end the slaughter.

3. Nothing is worth losing loved ones.

4. If we stop now, no more men will die.

Consider the nature of the setting in which Lincoln made his speech. Think of how persuasive he had to be, for he spoke in a graveyard over the bodies of 3,070 Union soldiers who had given their lives in one battle, fought just outside a small Pennsylvania town. Wounded in that battle were 14,497 men, and 5,437 more were captured or missing. Yet that little-known town is now arguably more famous because of Lincoln's brief "spoken essay" than it is because of the actual bloody battle fought there over a century ago.

The Argumentative Essay *(cont.)*

By addressing the people's deepest concerns, Lincoln must persuade those who want to stop the war to continue the "unfinished work." Argumentative writing is written to persuade, so it is constructed to talk to those who have opinions different from the writer's.

The Gettysburg Address

(Delivered in 1863 at the Consecration of the Gettysburg, Pennsylvania, Civil War Cemetery)

Four score and seven years ago our fathers brought forth on this continent a new nation, conceived in liberty and dedicated to the proposition that all men are created equal.

Now we are engaged in a great civil war, testing whether that nation or any nation so conceived and so dedicated can long endure. We are met on a great battlefield of that war. We have come to dedicate a portion of that field as a final resting place for those who gave their lives that that nation might live. It is altogether fitting and proper that we should do this.

But in a larger sense, we cannot dedicate—we cannot consecrate—we cannot hallow—this ground. The brave men, living and dead, who struggled here have consecrated it far above our poor power to add or detract. The world will little note nor long remember what we say here, but it can never forget what they did here. It is for us, the living, rather, to be dedicated here to the unfinished work which they who fought here have thus far so nobly advanced. It is rather for us to be here dedicated to the great task remaining before us—that from these honored dead we take increased devotion to that cause for which they gave the last full measure of devotion; that we here highly resolve that these dead shall not have died in vain; that this nation, under God, shall have a new birth of freedom; and that government of the people, by the people, for the people shall not perish from the earth.

—*Abraham Lincoln* (1809–1865)

Notice that Lincoln attempts to make his listeners understand that there is something even greater at stake here than lives of loved ones. He wants everyone to know that each person loyal to preserving the United States will be required to sacrifice his or her most precious gift. By doing this he is uniting the concerns and emotions of each person into a collective whole.

The Argumentative Essay *(cont.)*

Let's look at another famous speech given just a few years earlier than the Gettysburg Address. These are the words of Sojourner Truth, who was asking that her listeners look at her not as a black woman but as a woman. She further wants her listeners to consider the differences between men and women. Although Sojourner Truth speaks in nonstandard English, it doesn't take away from her effectiveness as a speaker. Consider that it might actually make her more effective.

Ain't I a Woman?

(Delivered in 1851 at the Women's Convention, Akron, Ohio)

Well, children, where there is so much racket there must be something out of kilter. I think that 'twixt the Negroes of the South and the women at the North, all talking about rights, the white men will be in a fix pretty soon. But what's all this here talking about?

That man over there says that women need to be helped into carriages, and lifted over ditches, and to have the best place everywhere. Nobody ever helps me into carriages, or over mud-puddles, or gives me any best place! And ain't I a woman? Look at me! Look at my arm? I have ploughed and planted, and gathered into barns, and no man could head me!

And ain't I a woman? I could work as much and eat as much as a man—when I could get it—and hear the lash as well!

And ain't I a woman? I have borne 13 children, and seen most all sold off to slavery, and when I cried out with my mother's grief, none but Jesus heard me! And ain't I a woman?

Then they talk about this thing in the head; what's this they call it? [member of audience whispers, "intellect"] That's it, honey. What's that got to do with women's rights or Negroes' rights? If my cup won't hold but a pint, and yours holds a quart, wouldn't you be mean not to let me have my little half-measure full?

Then the little man in black there, he says women can't have as much rights as men, 'cause Christ wasn't a woman! Where did your Christ come from? Where did your Christ come from? From God and a woman! Man had nothing to do with Him.

If the first woman God ever made was strong enough to turn the world upside down all alone, these women together ought to be able to turn it back, and get it right side up again! And now they is asking to do it, the men better let them.

Obliged to you for hearing me, and now old Sojourner ain't got nothing more to say.

—*Sojourner Truth (1797–1883)*

Standards and Benchmarks: 1A, 1D, 1F, 2C, 2D, 3A, 3I, 3J, 3K

The Argumentative Essay *(cont.)*

Imagine Sojourner Truth about to deliver a speech. She has only a very few minutes. What is running through her mind? She knows only a handful in the audience will agree with her, so she must make her words count. She considers how to move her listeners.

Make a pro-and-con chart of what Sojourner may have considered before her speech.

Pro

1. _____
2. _____
3. _____
4. _____

Con

1. _____
2. _____
3. _____
4. _____

Discuss your ideas in small groups or in a full class discussion.

Add any more pro and con statements here that you feel are worthy of consideration.

Pro

5. _____
6. _____

Con

5. _____
6. _____

Write what you think is the thesis of Sojourner Truth's speech.

_____

_____

_____

Standards and Benchmarks: 1A, 1F, 2B, 2C, 2D, 3A, 3F, 3G, 3I, 3J, 3K

The Argumentative Essay *(cont.)*

Look at the paragraph on page 122 about teenage smoking.

Make a pro and con sheet for this essay.

Pro	Con
1. _____ _____	1. _____ _____
2. _____ _____	2. _____ _____
3. _____ _____	3. _____ _____
4. _____ _____	4. _____ _____

Brainstorm as a group some subjects that concern your class. Now use one of the subjects that is interesting to you and develop a pro and con chart.

Subject: _____

Pro	Con
1. _____ _____	1. _____ _____
2. _____ _____	2. _____ _____
3. _____ _____	3. _____ _____
4. _____ _____	4. _____ _____

Use the chart to develop an argumentative essay. You may use the back of this page to write a first copy of your introductory (thesis statement) paragraph. If your teacher approves it, write the complete essay on another sheet of paper.

Standards and Benchmarks: 1A, 1B, 1D, 1E, 2B, 2C, 2D, 3A, 3I, 3J, 3K

The Argumentative Essay *(cont.)*

How is an argumentative paragraph different from a comparison-and-contrast paragraph? In comparison/contrast writing a writer is expected to discuss both sides of the thesis. In argumentative writing the writer is *not* required to discuss both sides. The job is to make the case for the side of the thesis you have chosen to discuss. Some student writers fall into the trap of not choosing one side over another. Here is an example of this problem.

> No one should have to take physical education in middle school unless they want to. The class takes away from what school is really about— improving your mind. The time on the field could be put to better use in the classroom. Most students use P.E. as a time to fool around and talk to their friends rather than learning about how to improve their physical skills. It is difficult for the teacher to attempt to keep students under control outside. It becomes a wasted hour every day. However, some students would get no exercise at all unless they had a physical education class.

Where does this writer go wrong? Yes, in the last sentence. This is an argumentative paragraph. It begins discussing the problems with taking physical education and should not change its focus. In comparison/contrast writing the writer can choose to explain both sides. However, in argumentative writing it is a mistake to mention the other side of the argument unless the writer is going to explain immediately why it is wrong.

How is this done? Let's take another look at the last sentence of the physical education paragraph and see what the writer could have done.

> It is true that some students would get no exercise at all unless they had a physical education class, but they would be better off joining a team after school since the majority of students don't use the class to improve their physical conditioning.

Can you think of other ways to close the paragraph? Try writing another solution on the lines below.

_____

_____

_____

_____

Standards and Benchmarks: 1B, 1E, 2B, 2C, 2D, 3A, 3I, 3K

The Argumentative Essay *(cont.)*

Read the following paragraph and revise or improve the sentences that discuss the opposite point of view. Don't leave the sentences out. Change them so they help the argument as modeled in the example given on page 132 in the paragraph about physical education. Write your revised paragraph in the space provided at the bottom of the page.

Cats make better pets than dogs. However, many people consider dogs to be more enjoyable. They do not require as much attention. It is common for pets to be left alone every day during the week for several hours while people are at work or school. Cats can usually entertain themselves while dogs need human attention to be happy. Dogs tend to be more loving than cats. Cats do not need to be cared for as much as dogs. You don't need to walk a cat. Most cats can spend their entire lives inside a house, but most dogs need outside recreation. It is fun to walk a dog around the neighborhood. Busy people who are considering a pet should make a cat their choice.

Revised Paragraph

_____

_____

_____

_____

_____

_____

_____

_____

_____

_____

Standards and Benchmarks: 1B, 1E, 2B, 2C, 2D, 3A, 3I, 3J, 3K

The Argumentative Essay *(cont.)*

Here is one way a student improved the paragraph about cats. How is it similar to yours? How is it different?

Cats make better pets than dogs. Many people think dogs are more enjoyable; however, if you have a busy lifestyle, a cat will be a better choice. They do not require as much attention. It is common for pets to be left alone every day during the week for several hours while people are at work or school. Cats can usually entertain themselves while dogs need human attention to be happy. While dogs tend to be more loving than cats, they can be very sad if left alone day after day. Cats do not need to be cared for as much as dogs. You don't need to walk a cat. Most cats can spend their entire lives inside a house, but most dogs need outside recreation. It is fun to walk a dog around the neighborhood but not when it is raining or snowing. Busy people who are considering a pet should make a cat their choice.

Consider the following argumentative paragraph. Revise the sentences by changing them to help the argument.

The best place to enjoy a family vacation is in a warm climate. Almost everyone enjoys a place where the weather is beautiful and clear. There might be those in the family who would prefer to go to the mountains in the winter. In the summer at the beach you can go swimming and diving. You can play many types of sports on the sand. Of course, you can't go skiing. It is comfortable to go around all day in T-shirts, shorts, and no shoes. Some people might complain that it gets too hot. If your family took a vote, it would choose a vacation where the weather is warm.

Revised Paragraph

_____

_____

_____

_____

_____

The Argumentative Essay *(cont.)*

Let's begin our practice of the argumentative essay by re-writing the essay on page 120 about teenage driving. Your purpose will be to explain the reasons it is a good idea for teenagers to get a driver's license. Before you begin, study the essay. Notice that the writer has chosen the following support.

1. expense of owning a car

2. parents expecting you to run errands you don't want to do

3. the emotional strain of getting into an accident

Now, what will be your support? Remember you want to persuade your reader that it is valuable for teenagers to drive. Consider the following: being helpful to family, getting to jobs, teaching responsibility and maturity. Your audience will include parents, so use arguments that will persuade mature readers.

Your thesis: _____

Your arguments:

1. _____

2. _____

3. _____

4. _____

Now write the essay, beginning below on this page and continuing on the back. When you are finished, give your essay a title and submit it to your teacher for response. Perhaps your teacher will want you to revise it.

_____

_____

_____

_____

_____

_____

_____

_____

Standards and Benchmarks: 1D, 2D

The Argumentative Essay *(cont.)*

Here is an example of a student's essay on the positive aspects of teenage driving. He used the essay on page 120 for his model.

Middle school students dream of the day they will be able to drive. The freedom of doing what you want is very exciting. Of course, parents are nervous about having their child behind the wheel, and there are important considerations concerning safety. However, having a teenager driving relieves the parent of many obligations, helps the student to learn responsibility, and allows the young driver to understand how to handle problems. There are many significant positive reasons parents should think about that make teenage driving an important experience for maturing.

Parents are so busy in today's world. They must work extra hours to meet their financial commitments. Having a teenage driver will help parents. The teenager can help pick up younger brothers and sisters from school or activities so parents won't have to rush home. The young driver can run errands like getting groceries. In an emergency there will another driver at home who can help. With each of these necessities, the teen driver can assist parents.

Taking care of a car will teach a teen responsibility. First, the teen will need to make sure the car is in good running condition. Second, he or she will learn to understand the importance of safe driving techniques. Finally, a driver must learn the rules of the road, and even a teen who might have been spoiled by thinking only of himself will soon recognize others first.

All drivers face problems, and this will help a teen mature. He might get a flat tire and have to deal with that emergency. He will have to learn how to find and follow directions. He will need to schedule his time so he arrives on time for appointments. Most importantly, he will learn that having privileges always comes with necessary duties. All of these are important adult lessons.

Parents may consider that having a car is too much responsibility for a teenager. However, it is actually a great way to teach responsibility. Parents want to teach their child to become an adult they can be proud of. Becoming a careful and concerned driver might be the very best way to acquire these adult qualities.

As a class discuss this essay.

1. What has the writer done well?

2. What improvements can be made? How would you title this essay?

3. Do you think he has written a convincing argumentative essay? Why or why not?

4. Has he used appropriate transitional words? List them on the board.

Standards and Benchmarks: 1A, 1B, 1D, 1E, 1F, 1J, 2B, 2C, 2D, 3A, 3I, 3J, 3K

The Argumentative Essay *(cont.)*

Now it is time to write your own argumentative essay.

Follow these steps:

I. Beginning

Begin by brainstorming some ideas in a group. One way many students have found useful is to use a newspaper. Each member of your group should take a different section of the paper—front section, editorial section, sports section, entertainment section, business section. Each member should have a highlighter. Scan your section for interesting articles. Highlight any headlines or article headings for subjects. Find at least five. Then, as a group, discuss which would make suitable topics. Then write possible thesis statements. Share the best thesis statements with the class.

II. Brainstorming

Use one or more of the brainstorming techniques you have worked with from this book or other places. Come up with some pro and con arguments. Try writing a couple of thesis paragraphs until you feel comfortable with one.

III. Drafting the Essay

Write a four- to five-paragraph essay. Don't try to write it all at once. Give yourself a couple of days before you feel satisfied with what you have. Revise as much as you can.

IV. Peer Reading

Have a member of your class read your essay as you read another's. Help that person by answering the questions on the next page.

V. Revising

Revise your essay using the peer reading comments.

VI. Evaluating

Hand in your revision to your teacher for evaluation. Make sure to hand in all sections so your teacher can see that you understand the writing process.

Standards and Benchmarks: 1D, 2B, 2C, 3A, 3I, 3J, 3K

Peer Checklist for Your Argumentative Essay

When you have finished the draft of your essay and have reread it to correct any obvious mistakes, give it to a classmate to read. The classmate is to read the essay carefully at least twice before answering the following.

Writer: _____

Date: _____

Reader: _____

1. What is the topic of the essay?

   _____

2. Is the topic argumentative? What could be the opposite argument?

   _____

3. What is the thesis of the essay? Write it down.

   _____

4. Can you understand the writer's view on his or her subject? Explain.

   _____

5. What are the main points the writer uses to support the thesis?

   A. _____

   B. _____

   C. _____

6. Does the writer try to answer the question(s) that someone with another view might have? Explain.

   _____

7. What transitions has the writer used? Write them down.

   _____

8. What are your suggestions for the writer so he or she might improve the essay?

   _____

   _____

Return the paper to the writer.

Technology Tips

More and more of your students are using computers. Just how useful present computer instructional programs are in helping to teach writing is still being debated. Here, however, are some specific ideas you might use to involve your students working with technology.

1. Show students how to use the grammar-check function in a word-processing program to ensure they have avoided sentence fragments and run-ons.

2. Have students use Internet search engines such as Yahoo! or Excite to research their topics for expository writing.

3. Have students go online to your local newspaper's Web site for editorial columns they can use for argumentative writing.

4. Have students practice their e-mail skills by sending messages to friends to ask their opinions and seek help to support their essay topics.

5. Create graphic organizers using computer programs such as *Student Writing Center* or *Inspiration.*

6. Have students research a particular subject on the Internet and use a double-column graphic organizer to take notes.

7. Use a digital camera to take pictures that illustrate students' topics. Include pictures as part of the assignment.

8. Have students compose at the computer and use the cut-and-paste functions of a word processing program to organize details in different ways.

9. Have students use the thesaurus function to come up with alternative words that might better suit their meanings.

10. Work with students in the word processing program to revise their use of transitional words.

11. Work with the grammar-check function to make sure students have used correct subject-verb agreement throughout their essays. (Some word processing programs provide automatic highlighting of passive voice constructions. This feature gives the teacher a good opportunity to teach this construction to the class and demonstrate when it is appropriate and when it is not. This will help you show students how to improve their writing by normally avoiding such expressions.)

Technology Tips *(cont.)*

12. Have students post their expository essays on the school's Web site.

13. Have students practice their use of the attachment function of e-mail by sending their essays to their home computers.

14. Using the attachment function, send a copy of a student essay to a friend, relative, or political figure.

15. Practice using a scanner to include illustrations of students' subjects.

16. Have students practice using different fonts for their essays. Discuss why certain fonts and sizes are not appropriate for expository writing. Select, as a class, the two or three fonts that are acceptable for the class to use.

17. Practice using the underline, bold, and italics functions. Discuss when these are appropriate to use in expository writing.

18. Have students explore Newsgroups, which are discussion groups that can be found on the Usenet (the Users network). These sites can be located by using a search engine. Also try the NetNews Overview Index. These sites are divided into hierarchies such as *talk* (discussion of controversial subjects), *news* (updates in all genres of news), and *soc* (social issues). They can help your students with their expository topics and research.

19. Have students find e-mail sites for their favorite magazines. These could have valuable information they might use in their writing.

20. Start an e-mail pen pal site for your class with another school. Discuss uses for the site in connection with writing assignments.

Answer Key

Many activities in this book are subjective. For some activities at the beginning of the book, the teacher is provided with "possible answers" to serve as guides. In most cases, however, the notation "Answers will vary" will appear in the key.

Page 24

1. The topic is "Mrs. Smith was one of my favorite teachers."

2. The controlling idea is "she went out of the way to help me when I was having trouble with math."

3. The three main supporting ideas are:

    (1) Mrs. Smith would come in early to help.

    (2) She would think of activities involving food.

    (3) She would go over a lesson again but not embarrass me.

4. *Answers will vary.*

Page 25

1. <u>Smoking cigarettes</u> is (harmful to your health.)

2. <u>Taking the train</u> can (save money.)

3. <u>Our state capitol building</u> is one of the most (beautiful in the country.)

4. <u>Sandra is a high school student</u> who is talented but (quite shy.)

5. The <u>best tennis players</u> need to be (graceful.)

6. <u>Most students who want jobs</u> must (wait until they are 16.)

7. <u>Changing dollars into foreign currency</u> can be (confusing.)

8. <u>Developing computer skills </u>will (help you in high school.)

9. <u>Juan can eat more than anyone in our family</u>, but he (never gains weight.)

10. <u>Hiking in the woods</u> is (dangerous.)

(Support sentence answers will vary.)

Page 26

2. The children in *The Sound of Music* make it a delightful film.

3. New York is too crowded.

6. K-Mart is a good place to shop if you are on a budget.

8. Studying Latin will also help you learn many difficult English words.

10. Kodiak bears are dangerous for campers in Alaska.

(Explanations will vary.)

Page 27—*Possible Answers:*

2. A school field trip to the zoo will make learning about animals more exciting.

3. The movie had a fascinating story about the problems of a one-parent family.

4. Swimming will help you lose weight.

5. Cats make great pets since they enjoy spending time alone.

6. Thanksgiving is the best holiday because our family has wonderful traditions.

7. My friend, Beth, would make a great president since she has great organizational abilities.

8. Skateboarding without a helmet and proper equipment is dangerous.

9. Adults may disapprove of skateboarding if done among pedestrians.

10. School rules about common courtesy seem unnecessary.

Page 29

1. [After Sam and Pete arrived,] (we began the meeting.)

2. (The teacher asked me to read) [since I have the loudest voice.]

3. (English and social studies are easy for me) [although, math is hard.]

4. [Unless you explain the problem carefully,] (no one will be able to understand it.)

5. (The ocean should be calm today) [unless there is a storm.]

6. [When the lightning began,] (the lifeguards made everyone come out of the water.)

7. [Before my sister was born,] (I was the only child in the house.)

8. (You will stay cool) [if you do not run around in the hot sun.]

9. (I like to sing,) [even though no one likes to hear me.]

10. (The house on the corner has the most beautiful garden) [because the owners work on it every weekend.]

Answer Key (cont.)

Page 30—*Possible Answers:*

1. Sam turned bright red when everyone made fun of him.
2. Unless the sun comes out, the class picnic will be cancelled.
3. Until someone turned on the lights, no one would know she was there.
4. Celia could not play one tune on the piano before she took lessons.
5. I had to take back the coat my grandmother sent me because it was the wrong color.
6.–15. Answers will vary.

Page 33—*Possible Answers:*

1. I want to run, but she wants to walk.
2. When the car went over the cliff, it was still burning.
3. Martha came to my house, and she explained the homework to me.
4. After the class heard the last bell, they ran quickly out of the room.
5. Tom will go to a movie, or he can rent one.
6. The parade float turned the corner while the police stopped the traffic.
7. Simon has made many friends, although he has only been here two months.
8. The corn plants grew tall since we took good care of them all winter.
9. My neighbors will go on vacation to Costa Rica, and they will visit their relatives in Mexico.
10. My parents hate my new shoes, but I love them!

(Reverse Corrections: Answers will vary.)

Page 34—*Possible Construction:*

When Mrs. Clay was a little girl in the 1950s, she celebrated her birthdays with her family. She loved parties, but some things about them bothered her. She always thought it was unfair to get so many presents since she knew many children in her community never got anything. Every passing year brought Mrs. Clay more concern. Now Mrs. Clay celebrates her birthdays at a local children's home. She gets some presents, and she gives some presents. She thinks this is a meaningful celebration for her family since it shows them that others need their support. Her son, Michael, saves up a part of his allowance all year, and he buys gifts for the homeless children. Although the Clay family is trying to persuade others to have their parties at the home, so far they have not been successful.

Page 35—*Possible Solution:*

After Sandra lived in New York City for ten years, she moved to the country last March. She likes living in the country, but sometimes she likes the excitement of the city. There are no movies or plays in her little town, so she goes back to New York every three months. She also visits some old friends, although Sandra's best friend, Adriana, would rather visit her. Adriana likes the quiet in Sandra's town, and she often takes long walks in the woods. Adriana likes seeing all the animals, and horseback riding is one activity she never fails to do. Sometimes Adriana thinks the wrong person moved to the country, but Sandra says she will never move back to New York City.

Page 48—*Possible Answers:*

1. The opinion is that holding a school office will bring rewards. It's found in the last sentence in paragraph.
2. Controlling ideas:

   Paragraph 2—Some people enjoy being in the center of school activities.

   Paragraph 3—People who want to be student officers like to feel they are in command.

   Paragraph 4—Participation in school government will be positive when getting to high school or applying for a job.
3. The last paragraph sums up the essay by repeating the major points of the essay.
4. social connections, helping school and community, learning about politics
5. takes too much time, must forget other activities, no time for old friends, being snobbish or conceited
6. Holding a school office often changes a person for the worse.

Page 51—*Sample Answers:*

1. An after-school job will help pay for school expenses. An after-school job will make the student stay up too late at night finishing his homework.
2. If I had the opportunity to go anywhere in the world, I would choose Italy with its beautiful scenery. If I could go anywhere in the world, I would stay near home and visit the beautiful northern part of the state.
3. The most beautiful season of the year is winter when snow makes the whole city clean and white. I like summer best when there is no school and the days are long with so much to do.

4, 5, 6. (Answers will vary.)

Page 53

1, 2, 4, 6, 9, 10—no

3, 5, 7, 8—yes

Answer Key *(cont.)*

Page 54—*Possible Answers:*

2. Learning a foreign language is difficult, but the rewards are many.

3. There are not enough basketball courts or soccer fields in our city for all the people who enjoy playing these sports.

4. The advantages of living in an apartment are many, especially for people who have small children.

5. The Internet is a tremendous waste of time if you are just browsing.

6, 7, 8, 9, 10. *(Answers will vary.)*

Page 56—*Possible Answers:*

1. There are many exceptional reasons for a family to own a dog.

2. A city could not survive without police officers.

3. Restaurants provide many services for their customers.

Page 59

Although each paragraph will be unique, be sure that the students are writing cohesively. Here is an example for the first one:

All schools can use improvement, and ours is no different. There are not enough fields for soccer and baseball. Also, many students cannot find a place to sit at lunch. The classrooms are crowded already, and desks are being added all the time. It is time that the school board makes plans to create more room by building on the empty lot next door to the west side of the school.

Page 64—*Possible Answers:*

1. The topic is about watching TV. The controlling idea is that watching TV is a waste of time.

2. Controlling idea #1—steals the opportunity to do the best job on your school work.

   Controlling idea #2—gives the chance to put off chores you promised to complete.

   Controlling idea #3—takes away the opportunity to communicate with those around you.

3. The writer proves her point since she has many examples of why she feels as she does. *(Agreement or disagreement will vary.)*

4. Many TV programs provide knowledge not easily found anywhere else.

   Many families find that not having a TV in their home actually creates more time for all the members.

   If there is only one TV in the home, then a family can be together watching and then discussing the program.

Page 65—*Sample Concluding Paragraph*

San Francisco has many types of food that visitors enjoy. Whether you go to Chinatown for the best Chinese food outside of China, visit North Beach for meals from authentic Italian regions, or wander to Fisherman's Wharf for a San Francisco specialty, everyone will find something to enjoy. Many tourists make repeated trips to this great city to sample its more than one-hundred different types of food.

Pages 69 and 70

1. Restaurants in San Francisco

2. Restaurants are found in their own special areas.

   "The restaurant locations in the special neighborhoods of San Francisco make the experience of dining very special."

3. Chinese food, Italian food, seafood

4. There are Chinese temples, opera houses, and fishing boats by the eating places.

5. Walk down Lombard Street and climb Telegraph Hill to work up an appetite.

6. Ahi tuna, octopus, or eel.

7. They are the very ships that catch the fish you eat.

8. The unique combination of smells of fish, bay, and sourdough bread.

9. Answers will vary (e.g., smells make for lasting memories).

10. More Chinese live in San Francisco's Chinatown than in any other single community outside of China.

11. It is the last sentence in the paragraph.

12. *(Answers will vary.)*

Pages 73 and 74

(Answers will vary.)

Page 75

1. First

2. Second

3. Third

4. Next

5. Last

Page 76

1, 4, 3, 2

Answer Key *(cont.)*

Page 77

By, Then, Next, Before, At, Then, After, Finally

Page 78

(Answers will vary.)

Page 79

By, until, During, before, in

Page 87

(Answers will vary.)

Page 100

1. Topic: Remembering the old home in Vietnam

   Controlling Idea: What I remember and what is real are not the same.

2. He remembers a beautiful yellow house, strong walls, a curtained window, light blue covering, and a place for playing marbles and soccer outside the window. He now sees crumbling walls in need of paint, a broken window with no curtain, and a muddy hole where he once played. What is remembered is beautiful, but what is real is ugly.

3. His memories of climbing the tree for escape, imaginative fancy of a super hero, and cool breezes are contrasted with the ugly bundle of branches, scarred trunk, and diseased appearance.

4. Reality and memory are far apart.

5. He would rather have the pleasant memories of the past than the knowledge of ugly reality of the present.

Page 102

1. Contrast: Differences rather than similarities are stressed.

2. Topic: Physical conditioning in soccer and football

   Controlling Idea: Soccer requires better conditioning than football.

3. A. Soccer players must run continually, but football players get to stop after each play.

   B. Soccer players must remain slim and agile while football players put on bulk.

   C. Soccer players play several games per week while football player play only one game per week.

4. Soccer requires better conditioning.

5. Soccer and football conditioning needs.

6, 7. *(Answers will vary.)*

Page 111

(Answers will vary.)

Page 121

1. "Although most middle school students dream of the day they will get a driver's license, there are many nightmares they might not consider which come with that 'wonderful' document."

2. They think it will be fun.

3, 4, 5, 6. *(Answers will vary.)*

Page 123

Numbers 2, 3, 4, 7, and 8 should have an X placed beside them.

Page 124

Numbers 1, 3, 6, and 9 should have "No" written beside them.

Numbers 2, 4, 5, 7, 8, and 10 should have an A written beside them.